GRAMMAR AND BEYOND

WORKBOOK

Laurie Blass
Barbara Denman
Susan Iannuzzi

4

CAMBRIDGE
UNIVERSITY PRESS

CAMBRIDGE UNIVERSITY PRESS
Cambridge, New York, Melbourne, Madrid, Cape Town,
Singapore, São Paulo, Delhi, Mexico City

Cambridge University Press
32 Avenue of the Americas, New York, NY 10013-2473, USA

www.cambridge.org
Information on this title: www.cambridge.org/9781107604094

© Cambridge University Press 2013

First published 2013

Printed in the United States of America

A catalog record for this publication is available from the British Library.

ISBN 978-0-521-14301-1   Student's Book 4
ISBN 978-0-521-14323-3   Student's Book 4A
ISBN 978-0-521-14328-8   Student's Book 4B
ISBN 978-1-107-60409-4   Workbook 4
ISBN 978-1-107-60410-0   Workbook 4A
ISBN 978-1-107-60411-7   Workbook 4B
ISBN 978-1-107-67297-0   Teacher Support Resource Book with CD-ROM 4
ISBN 978-0-521-14343-1   Class Audio CD 4
ISBN 978-1-139-06188-9   Writing Skills Interactive 4

Art direction and layout services: Integra
Editorial management: Hyphen S.A.

Contents

PART 2 Comparison and Contrast | Human Behavior

PART 3 Narrative | Society and Culture

PART 6 Summary–Response and Persuasion | Social Issues and Technology

Art Credits

Illustration

Bill Dickson: 151; **Rob Schuster:** 4; **Matt Stevens:** 96;
Richard Williams: 49, 104

Photography

6 ©Jonio Machado/Age Fotostock; 13 ©iStockphoto/Thinkstock; 19 ©Vladimir Godnik/Getty Images; 30 ©Martin San/Stone/Getty Images; 36 ©Palmi Gudmundsson/Nordic Photos/Getty Images; 39 ©Paul Williams/Alamy; 44 ©Medioimages/Photodisc/Getty Images; 55 ©Ghislain & Marie Davi/Cultura/Age Fotostock; 56 ©Ilya Terentyev/Vetta/Getty Images; 60 ©Lance King/Getty Images Sport/Getty Images; 66 ©Jeremy Woodhouse/Blend Images/Getty Images; 72 ©Redchopsticks/Getty Images; 78 ©Don Cravens/Time & Life Pictures/Getty Images; 79 *(all)* ©Time Life Pictures/Getty Images; 80 ©Hulton Collection/Getty Images; 86 ©PhotoQuest/Archive Photos/Getty Images; 90 ©DreamPictures/The Image Bank/Getty Images; 94 ©Commercial Eye/Stockbyte/Getty Images; 109 ©Zero Creatives/Cultura/Getty Images; 110 ©Eric Audras/PhotoAlto Agency RF Collections/Getty Images; 115 ©Thomas Kitchin & Victoria Hurst/First Light/Getty Images; 116 ©Dinodia Photos/Alamy; 117 ©Fuse/Getty Images; 120 ©Mark Andersen/Rubberball/Getty Images; 124 ©Stockbyte/Getty Images; 132 ©Radius Images/Alamy; 134 ©Larry Williams/Blend Images/Getty Images; 138 ©Richard Green/Commercial/Alamy; 143 ©Michael Rosenfeld/Getty Images; 153 ©Photodisc/Thinkstock; 175 ©Chris Ryan/OJO Images/Getty Images; 177 ©SimoJarratt/Corbis Super RF/Alamy

Cause and Effect 1

The Environment and You

Sentence Structure: Simple and Compound Sentences

1 Read the paragraph about the environment. Then label the words in bold in each sentence.

> S = subject   V = verb   OBJ = object

сывотки

Contraction

_S_ **Human activity** has an impact on the natural environment. We all know that.
(1)

However, this __V__ **doesn't have to spell** disaster! There are many ways in which we
(2)

can contribute to a brighter future for the Earth. One way is to reduce __OBJ__ **the use**
(3)

of plastics. Manufacturing less plastic lessens __S__ **the consumption of natural**
(4)

resources. __S__ **Petroleum and natural gas** are two of the main constituents of plastic.
(5)

чанишашиеи

Individuals can minimize __OBJ__ **their consumption of plastics**. For instance, we __V__
(6)   (7)

can give store clerks our own reusable bags for our purchases. We can also try to use less

__OBJ__ **plastic wrap** for food storage. Through our purchasing decisions, we __V__ **can show**
(8)   (9)

manufacturers that we prefer products that are not packaged in a lot of plastic. Many __S__
(10)

supermarkets now offer places to recycle plastic bags, while others give shoppers credit

for using their own bags. __S__ **Deciding to take an active part in schemes like these** is
(11)

just one way that we can make the world a greener place for everyone.

2 Read each sentence. Then match the words in bold with the parts of speech.

a. **Using** renewable energy is a priority.

b. **Minor changes** can make a significant difference.

c. **Companies and individuals** need to work
   together on a solution.

d. **This** means playing an active role in recycling.

e. **The companies that care about the future of our
   planet** are those whose products we should buy.

f. **The future of the Earth** is in our hands.

1. Adjective + noun _b_

2. Pronoun _d_

3. Noun + noun _c_

4. Noun + prepositional phrase _f_

5. Noun + relative clause _e_

6. Gerund _a_

3 Complete the following sentences with the words in the box. Add commas and semicolons when necessary.

and	as a result	consequently	furthermore	however	~~so~~

1. Cars release carbon dioxide into the environment _, so_ try not to make unnecessary road trips.

2. Most people cannot give up their cars _; however ,_ they can choose to buy hybrid, fuel-efficient cars.

3. It's a good idea to combine trips instead of going out multiple times _, and_ carpooling with neighbors or co-workers saves gas.

4. A well-maintained car performs better and reduces emissions _; furthermore,_ it won't break down so often!

5. Biodiesel fuel, which some cars use, is made from plants _, and_ it is a renewable energy source.

6. More and more people are cycling to work. _Consequently ,_ the air is cleaner and people are fitter.

4 Correct the run-on sentences and comma splices. Use a comma and a coordinating conjunction, or use a period between the two independent clauses.

1. Being "green" isn't difficult more and more people are doing it.

   Being "green" isn't difficult, and more and more people are doing it.

2. Some companies are going paperless, employees send e-mails instead of letters.
   _so_
   _____

3. Telecommuting is becoming popular, working from home saves energy.
   for
   _____

4. Telecommuting means less travel less travel means less pollution.
   and
   _____

5. A hundred years ago, no one recycled, most of us do these days.
   but
   _____

6. In every city there are recycling facilities it's easy to recycle.
   _so_
   _____

Complex Sentences

1 Read the paragraph about climate change. Then label the words in bold in each sentence.

IC = independent clause   DC = dependent clause

IC (1) **Scientists use the term** *climate change* **to refer to major changes in weather lasting for two or more decades,** *DC* (2) **because it is more accurate than the term** *global warming*. *DC* (3) **Although some climate change is caused by natural changes in the sun or the atmosphere,** *IC* (4) **human-caused climate change is a growing concern.** The rate of change caused by human activities is increasing; *IC* (5) **the last decade has been the warmest on record.** *IC* (6) **Scientists are worried** about how fast climate change will happen in the future. *IC* (7) **Humans cause climate change** *DC* (8) **when they burn fossil fuels, cut down forests, and develop land.** *DC* (9) **As these activities release gases upward,** *IC* (10) **the atmosphere traps and holds their heat and warms the Earth.**

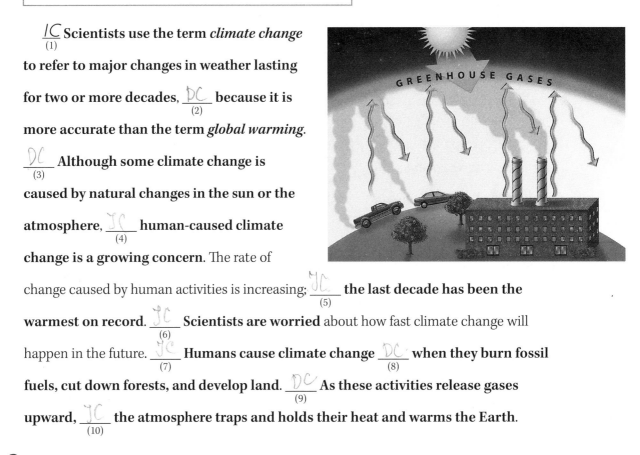

2 Complete the sentences about ways to reduce your ecological footprint. Use a subordinating conjunction in the box. Some words may be used more than once.

| although | because | if | since | whereas | whether |

1. *Because* hybrid cars are now easily available, people are switching to them.

2. People should walk to work __if__ they want to reduce their ecological footprint.

3. *Because* most people don't like to waste food, they are buying food more carefully than they used to.

4. Car buyers should choose more fuel-efficient vehicles, _although_ they may cost more.

5. Some companies are going green, _whereas_ others are not yet.

6. Telecommuting is often an option for workers, _because_ communication technology has improved so much.

7. _Whether_ it's called *global warming* or *climate change*, the fact remains that it's a worldwide problem.

3 A Read the sentences about the impact food has on the environment. Then label the items in each set as *C* (cause) or *E* (effect).

1. a. __C__ Natural resources are consumed to produce food.

   b. __E__ Many people are thinking harder about their food choices.

2. a. __C__ Fruits and vegetables are often grown far from where consumers buy them.

   b. __E__ They have to be transported many miles.

3. a. __E__ Food transportation contributes to climate change.

   b. __C__ The vehicles that transport products release dangerous gases into the air.

4. a. __C__ Many people today are concerned about the environmental effects of their food choices.

   b. __E__ They look for ways to reduce the ecological footprint of their food.

5. a. __E__ Some people are reducing the amount of meat in their diets.

   b. __C__ Raising animals for meat contributes to greenhouse gases.

6. a. __C__ Growing one's own produce can cut down on one's ecological footprint.

   b. __E__ Planting a vegetable garden has become increasingly popular.

B Combine the sentences from A into complex sentences showing cause and effect. Circle the correct word or phrase.

1. _____ natural resources are consumed to produce food, many people are thinking harder about their food choices.

   (a.) Because   b. Whether   c. After

2. _____ fruits and vegetables are grown far from the places where consumers buy them, they have to be transported many miles.

   a. Before   (b.) Although   c. If

3. Food transportation contributes to climate change _____ the vehicles that transport products release dangerous gases into the air.

   a. while   (b.) because   c. that

4. _____ people are concerned about the environmental effects of their food choices, they look for ways to reduce the ecological footprint of their food.

   (a.) Whereas   b. Whether   (c.) When

5. _____ raising animals for meat contributes to greenhouse gases, some people are reducing the amount of meat in their diets.

   (a.) Since   b. As if   c. After

6. Planting a vegetable garden has become increasingly popular _____ growing one's own produce can cut down on one's ecological footprint.

   a. because   b. after   (c.) while

Common Patterns with Nouns That Show Cause

1 Unscramble the words to complete the sentences about forest loss. Add punctuation when necessary.

1. of forest loss / and the burning of trees / are major causes / land development

   Land development and the burning of trees are major causes of forest loss.

2. agricultural land for crops / is the need for / cause of forest loss / another important

   _____

   _____

3. in richer countries is / the loss of forests / large ecological footprints / the primary cause of

   _____

   _____

4. less well-off countries / can be a root cause of / the lifestyles in richer countries / ecological problems in

   _____

   _____

5. the underlying causes / governments that focus on the / may miss / obvious causes of deforestation

   _____

6. leading causes of / economic and social policies / forest loss / are also

   _____

7. not the only cause / agriculture is probably / but it is / the leading cause of deforestation

   _____

2 Rewrite the sentences with the phrases below.

1. Resources are easily accessible; that's why people in some countries use so many resources.

   A major reason _people in some countries use so many resources_ is that _these resources are easily accessible_ .

2. Natural changes cause changes to the Earth's climate.

   One reason for _natural changes cause_ is _changes to the Earth's climate._ .

3. Our use of resources has increased; climate change has increased.

   The main reason _climate change has ↑_ is that _our use of resources has ↑_ .

4. Individuals' actions have consequences; people should think about their actions.

   The most important reason _people should think about their act._ is that _individual's actions have cons._ .

5. Making an estimate of one's ecological footprint can be helpful; it can help in making changes.

   The biggest reason _____ is that _____ .

6. Environmental organizations can be effective; as a result, many people support environmental organizations.

   The primary reason _____ is that _____ .

7. People are more interested in protecting the environment, which makes people participate in neighborhood cleanup days.

   One reason _____ is _____ .

3 Complete the sentences with *cause of*, *factor*, or *reason*.

1. Indoor air pollution can be a _cause of_ health problems.

2. A major _reason_ indoor air pollution is people smoking.

3. One _factor_ people should check indoor appliances is that it can prevent health problems.

4. The use of household chemicals is another critical _reason_ in indoor air pollution.

5. This is the _cause of_ why many people use natural cleaners at home.

6. Outside air can reduce the pollution in a home; for this _reason_ , opening windows can help.

7. Poor indoor air is a key _factor_ in allergy problems children suffer at school.

4 Complete the sentences. Use your own ideas.

1. One important cause of environmental problems is *human's actions according to nature and using a lot of chemicals in their life.*

2. The key factors countries worldwide need to address are *that environmental pollution is one of the main problems in our time.*

3. *Missaplication of chemicals and a security breach* is a leading cause of *many fatalities to extinguish a fire at a nuclear power station.*

4. One reason it can be difficult for countries to agree on environmental issues is that _____
_____.

Avoid Common Mistakes

1 Circle the mistakes.

1. **Today**, 80 percent of the **pollution in** the world's (**oceans from**) the land.
   (a)   (b)   (c)

2. One very significant **cause** of water pollution **runoff**, or chemicals that
                      (a)   (b)
   come from the land.
   (c)

3. Vehicles are a major (**because**) of runoff; **they leave** small amounts of oil on the
                           (a)   (b)
   roads every day.
   (c)

4. Rain and **snow this** oil to the rivers, **and** over time, **it washes** into the oceans.
            (a)   (b)   (c)

5. Another (**because**) of water pollution **is** air pollution **falling** from the air into rivers
           (a)   (b)   (c)
   and lakes.

6. (**And**) dirt and soil from farms or **from construction** can **cause** pollution if they wash
      (a)   (b)   (c)
   into the ocean.

7. Chemicals used **on farms or in yards** also **cause** water pollution (**when wash**)
                    (a)   (b)   (c)
   into the sea.

8. Every year, **fish and shellfish are** harmed (**cuz**) of pollution **in their** environments.
            (a)   (b)   (c)

2 Identify the common mistakes in the sentences. Label each sentence with the type of mistake from the box. If there is no mistake, write *e*. Then correct each sentence.

a. The sentence is a fragment.	d. Avoid beginning sentences with *And* and *But*.
b. Use *because*, not *coz* or *cuz*.	
c. Do not confuse *cause* with *because*.	e. There is no mistake.

_e_ One significant cause of ocean pollution is the accidental spilling of crude oil by
(1)
large, ocean-going ships. ____ The consequences of oil spills disastrous to both plant
(2)
and animal marine life. ____ For example, oil that spills on the surface of the water
(3)
blocks oxygen to marine plant life. ____ Marine plants require oxygen to live, and cuz
(4)
of oil on the surface of the water, they cannot access the oxygen that is necessary for
survival. ____ When this happens, marine plants. ____ Oil can because birds and
(5)   (6)
animals to lose their ability to stay warm and dry; as a result, they can die. ____ And oil
(7)
can also cause serious health problems in fish and in their eggs. ____ When sea birds
(8)
and animals try to clean themselves, they may die cause the oil they consume can be
poisonous. ____ After an oil spill, many veterinarians are needed to help clean birds and
(9)
animals who have come into contact with the oil. ____ Once they clean, the animals
(10)
can be returned to the environment. ____ But they are still in danger if the oil is still in
(11)
the water.

Self-Assessment

Circle the word or phrase that correctly completes each sentence.

1. An ecological _____ an estimate of the resources a person or group is consuming.

   a. footprint,   b. footprint is   c. footprint;

2. Buying local products reduces the need for _____ it reduces pollution.

   a. transportation so   b. transportation, but   c. transportation, so

3. Polluted bodies of water are unsafe, _____ humans should not use them for drinking water.

   a. when   b. so   c. although

4. People can save energy by using less, _____ they can use renewable sources of energy.

   a. but   b. or   c. so

5. Renewable energy isn't used as widely as nonrenewable _____ however, interest has grown as we have learned more about climate change.

   a. energy as   b. energy;   c. energy.

6. Although the Earth can produce more oil and _____ these resources cannot be renewed quickly.

   a. gas,   b. gas but   c. gas, but

7. The climate will continue to _____ greenhouse gas emissions aren't reduced.

   a. change if,   b. change if   c. change, if

8. Electric cars are one possible solution _____ they use fewer resources.

   a. because   b. as if   c. when

9. The main _____ the Earth's climate is changing so fast is human activity.

   a. cause   b. effect   c. reason

10. Burning oil and gas heats the Earth's atmosphere; for this _____ , ice at the Earth's poles is melting.

    a. reason   b. factor   c. cause

11. Resources are overused. _____ climate change is increasing.

    a. However,   b. Consequently,   c. Because

12. The Earth has a limited supply of resources like oil and gas and cannot quickly create _____ a result, environmentalists are concerned.

    a. more as   b. more; as   c. more as;

13. Scientists are researching other forms of energy _____ oil and gas are limited.

    a. cause   b. because   c. cuz

14. Many schools now have environmental education programs; _____ children are learning how our actions affect the Earth.

    a. furthermore   b. a result   c. consequently,

15. _____ some damage has been done to the Earth, it's not too late to take action.

    a. As if   b. Although   c. Consequently

Cause and Effect 2
Consumer Behavior

Subordinators and Prepositions That Show Cause, Reason, or Purpose

1 Read the paragraph about consumer behavior. Then label the words in bold in each sentence.

IC = independent clause	DC = dependent clause	PP = prepositional phrase

IC **Consumers' buying habits can be influenced by their moods and emotions**
(1)

or by how they feel physically. For instance, consumers may shop differently at different

times _____ **because of** how they feel; they may spend more when they are anxious, or
(2)

when they are sad. A consumer's buying decisions might be different from one day to the

next _____ **due to** the weather or the news. _____ **Consumers can learn to recognize**
(3)   (4)

these influences so that they can make better buying decisions and save money. _____
(5)

Because the way consumers feel affects their buying, business owners plan their

stores and restaurants carefully. People may spend more _____ **as a result of** the business's
(6)

lighting, sound, and scent. A store or restaurant manager might play relaxing music _____
(7)

so that consumers will take their time shopping or eating. Since pleasant scents can

remind consumers of holidays or of favorite foods, _____ **retailers may try to bring those**
(8)

scents into their stores. _____ **Since consumers may not be aware of the effect these**
(9)

factors have on them, they may spend more than they intended in stores and restaurants

with an atmosphere they find attractive. As a result, _____ **business owners often pay**
(10)

close attention to design, mood, and atmosphere when planning a new retail business

or restaurant.

2 Circle the subordinators and prepositions in the web article. Label them *C/R* (cause/reason) or *P* (purpose).

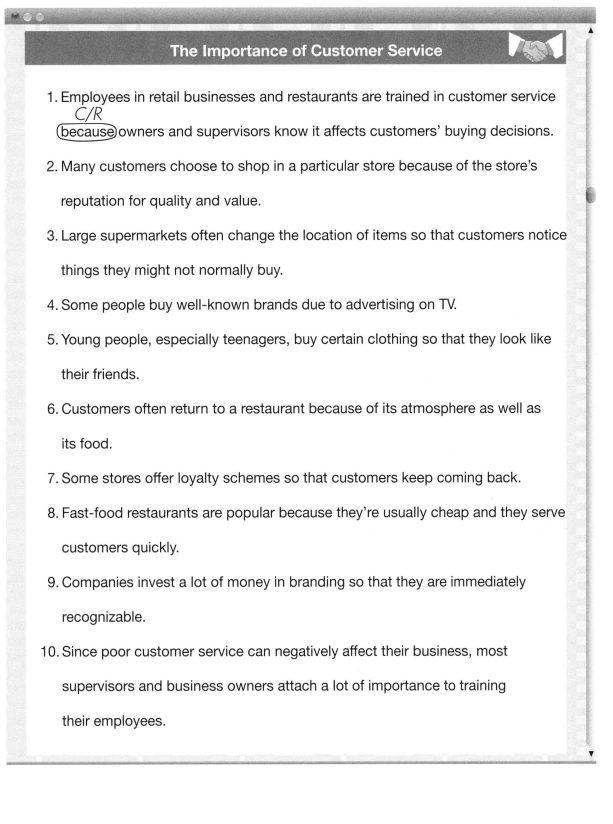

The Importance of Customer Service

1. Employees in retail businesses and restaurants are trained in customer service
   C/R
   (because) owners and supervisors know it affects customers' buying decisions.

2. Many customers choose to shop in a particular store because of the store's reputation for quality and value.

3. Large supermarkets often change the location of items so that customers notice things they might not normally buy.

4. Some people buy well-known brands due to advertising on TV.

5. Young people, especially teenagers, buy certain clothing so that they look like their friends.

6. Customers often return to a restaurant because of its atmosphere as well as its food.

7. Some stores offer loyalty schemes so that customers keep coming back.

8. Fast-food restaurants are popular because they're usually cheap and they serve customers quickly.

9. Companies invest a lot of money in branding so that they are immediately recognizable.

10. Since poor customer service can negatively affect their business, most supervisors and business owners attach a lot of importance to training their employees.

3 Complete the sentences about consumer buying habits. Circle the correct words or phrases.

1. (Because) / Because of people everywhere need to purchase food and household items, consumers tend to behave in the same way.

2. These days people are doing some of their food shopping online **due to / so that** competitive pricing and convenience.

3. **Due to / So** they can attract customers, some large stores have cafés and restaurants.

4. **So / Because** many people are very busy, they choose to eat at fast-food restaurants.

5. **So that / Since** advertising affects consumer choices, companies invest heavily in TV commercials.

6. Often shoppers buy items **because of / so** the way they are displayed.

7. Shoppers may not know that atmosphere, music, and scent can influence their decisions **due to / because** they do not always notice them.

8. Shoppers often make expensive purchases **as a result of / so that** the way a store displays items.

4 Complete the sentences about food shopping. Circle the word or phrase that correctly completes each sentence.

1. _____ food shopping can be one of a family's biggest expenses, it's important to shop wisely.

   a. So that   (b.)Because   c. Because of

2. Experts recommend making a list before shopping _____ you don't buy items you don't really need.

   a. since   b. due to   c. so that

3. They also recommend shopping after you have eaten to avoid overbuying _____ how hungry you feel.

   a. because   b. as a result   c. as a result of

4. _____ many stores put healthier foods around the outer edges of the store, experts recommend that consumers focus their shopping there.

   a. So that   b. Since   c. Due to

5. Health-conscious consumers avoid convenience foods _____ the fat and calories they contain.

   a. due to   b. because   c. so that

6. Large, bulk packages of food often appear cheaper _____ their size, but they may not be.

   a. because   b. because of   c. since

7. _____ the belief that coupons save money, some consumers use them to buy items they would not normally buy and do not need.

    a. As a result of   b. Since   c. So that

8. Consumers need to shop wisely _____ they can make the best choices for their health and budget.

    a. because   b. so that   c. due to

9. It is important to make wise purchasing decisions _____ the impact they can have on our financial future.

    a. so that   b. because   c. because of

5 Complete these sentences about consumer choices. Use your own ideas.

1. Food shopping in big stores takes time, so _____ .

2. Some people avoid eating fast food in order to _____ .

3. Others eat in fast-food restaurants because _____ .

4. Consumers are known to choose certain brands due to _____ .

5. Products are often chosen because of _____ .

6. Products are often discounted as a result of _____ .

Transition Words and Phrases That Show Effect

1 Read about the U.S. Federal Trade Commission (FTC). Then match each phrase or sentence with the phrase or sentence that would follow.

1. In the United States, the FTC makes rules that advertisers must follow. _d_

2. The FTC requires that advertisements be truthful; as a consequence, _____

3. Children are usually less knowledgeable than adults. _____

4. Advertisers are allowed to compare their product to another company's product. _____

5. Health and safety are especially important. _____

6. Ads may not leave out important information. _____

7. Ads that include statements about a product by an individual must be honest. As a result, _____

a. Consequently, the FTC closely watches safety claims and ads for health products.

b. As a result, ads sometimes mention other products by name.

c. Therefore, if an ad is for a computer but includes a picture of a printer, the ad must say, "Printer not included."

_d_. As a result, U.S. consumers have some protections.

e. advertisers must be sure not to give false information in their claims.

f. if a famous person has been paid to endorse a product, the advertiser must say so.

g. Thus, the FTC looks very carefully at ads that target children.

2 Unscramble the sentences about green products. Add punctuation when necessary.

1. they're called "green" products / therefore / help protect the Earth / environmentally responsible products

    Environmentally responsible products help protect the Earth; therefore,

    they're called "green" products.

2. look for green products / therefore, they / want to be environmentally conscious / some consumers

    _____

3. to attract these consumers / businesses want / they may look for green products to sell / as a result

    _____

4. be more expensive / consequently, they may / sometimes made from recycled items / green products are

    _____

5. they may have to make a difficult choice / as a consequence / consumers may care / about good prices and about the planet

    _____

6. they are also considered green products / can be used instead of more dangerous products / safe, natural household items like vinegar / therefore

    _____

7. businesses have responded to this aspect of the environmental movement / thus / in green products among consumers / there is a lot of interest

    _____

8. as a result / there are more and more / consumer demand for green products has increased / green products available

    _____

3 Complete the sentences about self-image. Use your own ideas.

1. Some people's self-image leads them to want to appear wealthy even if they are not. As

    a result, _____

    _____ .

2. For others, it's important to have the most up-to-date items; consequently,

    _____

    _____ .

3. Many people make choices because of what people in their social network do. Therefore,

   _____

   _____ .

4. In contrast, other people want to look and be different from everyone else; as a result,

   _____

   _____ .

Common Patterns with Nouns That Show Effect

1 Complete the paragraph about brands. Use the words and phrases in the box. You will use some words or phrases more than once.

effect	effects	result	results

Consumers' ideas about a product or food item have an *effect* on their buying
(1)
decisions. These decisions are often a _____ of advertising. Advertising
(2)
can have many psychological _____ on our actions. One example is the
(3)
importance some consumers attach to name brands (a product or group of products

that has a name and is made by a particular company). The _____ of name
(4)
brand advertising on us are that we recognize these products when we shop, and that

we may think name brands are better than local or less well-known products. However,

one _____ of the costs of advertising for consumers is that name brands
(5)
are usually more expensive. When stores put their own names or brands on a package,

the _____ may be that the product is less expensive, and many consumers
(6)
prefer them. Although many people say that there is no difference between house brands

and name brands, or that name brands have no _____ on them, advertising
(7)
can lead some people to think that name brands are better quality. When people think

this, the _____ is that they will only buy name brands. Some house brands
(8)
have names or packages that look like name brands. This generally has a positive

_____ , as consumers may feel more comfortable buying them. It's important
(9)
for consumers to be aware of some of the psychological _____ of advertising
(10)
so that they can make good purchasing decisions.

2 Complete the sentences about advertising. Circle the phrase that correctly completes each sentence.

1. TV and the Internet _____ .

   (a) have an effect on consumers' purchases

   b. as a result of consumers' purchases

   c. resulting consumers' purchases

2. Some advertisements say that a low price is only available for a short time. When this happens, _____ .

   a. unneeded purchases by consumers

   b. the result may be unneeded purchases by consumers

   c. unneeded purchases by consumers have a result

3. When a lot of people learn about a new product at the same time, _____ .

   a. the result is the effect on the product, and it becomes unavailable

   b. the effect on the product can be unavailable

   c. the result may be that the product becomes unavailable due to such a high demand

4. New products can become very popular very quickly; _____ .

   a. this can have an effect on the availability of the product

   b. one effect on demand for the product

   c. as a result of more demand for the product

5. Overconsumption can be caused by psychological factors; it can also _____ .

   a. have a significant effect on sophisticated advertising techniques

   b. have an effect on sophisticated advertising techniques

   c. be the result of sophisticated advertising techniques

6. One effect of the Internet on shopping _____ .

   a. is that we can check others' opinions of an item before we buy it

   b. has resulted in checking others' opinions of an item before we buy it

   c. is the effect of others' opinions of an item

7. When children see an item or a food on TV in an advertisement that targets them, _____ .

    a. they have an effect on that product

    b. the result may be that they have a very strong interest in that product

    c. it is a result of their strong interest in that product

8. Some parents believe that limiting their children's TV watching _____ .

    a. can have a good effect on their children's behavior

    b. is a good effect of advertising on their children

    c. can be a good result of advertising on their children

3 Unscramble the sentences about children and advertising.

1. of advertising / effect / one / is increased sales

   One effect of advertising is increased sales.

2. seeing a commercial on TV / are frequently / consumers' choices / the result of

   _____

   _____

3. is known to have / young children / advertising on TV / a significant effect on

   _____

   _____

4. that they want / when / see a commercial / children / often the result is / the item being advertised

   _____

5. children / to purchase toys and clothes / is a direct result / asking their parents / of seeing TV commercials

   _____

6. often has a positive result for them / are aware / that advertising / toy manufacturers

   _____

7. parents feel pressured / one effect of advertising is that / to buy items they can't afford

   _____

8. on a family's budget / negative effects / advertising can therefore have

   _____

4 Complete the sentences about the effects of advertising. Write sentences that are true for you.

1. When I was _____ ,

   _____ had a big effect on me.

2. One effect on me was _____ .

3. Today, _____ has little effect on me.

4. One day in the future, I hope to _____ .

   I hope that this has a big effect on _____ .

Avoid Common Mistakes

1 Circle the mistakes.

1. The (results on) online shopping are numerous; it's had a big **effect** **on** consumers and
   (a)   (b)   (c)
   businesses.

2. Increased online advertising is a **result in** the growth of online shopping; this has had
                                      (a)
   an **effect** **on** almost every website you visit.
      (b)   (c)

3. "Individual advertising" is a **result** **of** new technology; one **affect** of this is ads based on
                                 (a)   (b)   (c)
   users' past purchases or searches.

4. **Because** popular online auctions, you can buy almost anything from home. The
   (a)
   competition in these online auctions can have a negative **effect** **on** consumers.
                                                            (b)   (c)

5. Online auctions have an **effect** **on** the way people shop; as a result **on** these auctions,
                           (a)   (b)   (c)
   people sometimes spend more than they intended to.

6. It's important to be aware of the **effect** an auction can have **in** your interest in an item;
                                     (a)   (b)
   overspending can be a **result of** auctions.
                         (c)

7. Online auctions are popular for buying and selling old items and provide a new way

   for small shops to do business; as a **result** **on** this, auctions can also have an effect **on**
                                        (a)   (b)   (c)
   prices for these items.

8. This has an **effect** on prices. They may be lower **as a result from** low overheads, or they
                (a)   (b)
   may be higher **because of** bidding wars.
                 (c)

2 Identify the common mistakes in the sentences. Label each sentence with the type of mistake from the box. If there is no mistake, write *d*. Then correct each sentence.

a. Do not confuse *affect* and *effect*.

b. Remember to use the correct preposition in expressions with *cause* , *result*, and *effect*.

c. Do not confuse *because* with *because of*.

d. There is no mistake.

In 2008, millions of U.S. households received tax rebates from the government. _a_ (1)

The rebates were expected to have a positive ~~affect~~ *effect* on the economy. _____ The average (2)

rebate was $958; as a result on this, many families had some extra money. _____ In (3)

2011, the government did a study on the affects the rebates had on those households'

spending. _____ According to the study, about half of the households who received (4)

a rebate used the extra money mostly to pay off debts because very high credit card

bills and loans. _____ About 30 percent of recipients spent their rebate, which had a (5)

positive effect in the economy. _____ About 17 percent put the money in savings, having (6)

a positive affect on the household, but not on the economy. _____ The government also (7)

looked at the data to see whether age or income level affected the way people used their

rebates. _____ People younger than 55 were more likely to use the rebates to pay off (8)

debt; people older than 55 saved more of the rebate. _____ Of people under the age of 25, (9)

only about 13 percent put most of the money into savings. _____ Interestingly, the study (10)

showed that income level had little effect of the way that people used the money.

Self-Assessment

Circle the word or phrase that correctly completes each sentence.

1. Consumer behavior is the result of psychological processes. _____ we may be unaware of why we shop the way we do.

   a. Consequently,   b. As a result of,   c. Because

2. Consumers may buy a particular food as a result _____ the way they felt the first time they ate it.

   a. of   b. in   c. from

3. Some consumers do not want to waste resources. _____ many consumers try to buy used items.

   a. Therefore,   b. Due to   c. Resulting in

4. Other consumers will only buy new things _____ they want better quality.

   a. due to   b. so that   c. because

5. Consumers should make sure they are well informed _____ they make wise purchases.

   a. because   b. so that   c. therefore

6. One good _____ being well informed is that informed shoppers can save a lot of money.

   a. reason   b. effect in   c. effect of

7. Effective marketing sells _____ advertisers do a lot of research to create effective ads.

   a. products Therefore,   b. products. Therefore   c. products; therefore,

8. Selling advertising space provides income for Web _____ , there are many online ads.

   a. pages; resulted   b. pages; as a result   c. pages; Thus

9. Some of our spending habits are _____ the economic situation we grew up in.

   a. the result of   b. affects   c. as a result,

10. One _____ of changes in the price of gas is that people change their driving habits.

    a. effects   b. effect   c. cause

11. When gas prices rise, _____ more interest in environmentally friendly cars.

    a. as a consequence   b. the result is   c. as a result of

12. Many factors have an _____ consumers' purchases.

    a. affect   b. effect in   c. effect on

13. The growth of consumer protection agencies has _____ . Advertisements today are more truthful.

    a. had a result   b. had a result on   c. had a result in

14. Understanding how advertising works can help consumers change their shopping behavior; _____ they will spend their money more wisely.

    a. because of   b. as a result,   c. therefore

15. _____ some people aren't careful, they may buy things they don't need.

    a. Because of   b. Due to   c. Because

UNIT 3

Cause and Effect 3
Social Responsibility

Present and Future Real Conditionals

1 Complete the sentences about Penny's Organic Market. Circle the clause that best completes each sentence.

1. If customers are looking for a socially responsible grocery store with ethical business practices, _____ .

   a. Penny's Organic Market will be a good place to shop

   b. Penny's Organic Market is a good place to shop

   c. Penny's Organic Market was a good place to shop

2. If customers have empty cans and bottles, _____ .

   a. they can recycle them at Penny's and get five cents for each one

   b. they recycled them at Penny's and got five cents for each one

   c. they will not recycle them at Penny's and get five cents for each one

3. Penny's also gives customers _____ .

   a. five cents if they bring their own bags to use for the items they buy

   b. five cents they bring their own bags to use for the items they buy

   c. five cents, if they bring their own bags to use for the items they buy

4. Penny's lets customers bring their own glass jars _____ .

   a. they want to refill an old container instead of buying a new one

   b. if they want to refill an old container instead of buying a new one

   c. if they will want to buy a new container

5. When Penny's has bread that hasn't been sold, _____ .

   a. they gave it to a homeless shelter the next morning

   b. they will give it to a homeless shelter tomorrow

   c. they give it to a homeless shelter the next morning

6. Penny's donates food to community organizations _____ .

    a. whenever they are conducting a health fair or a cultural event

    b. if there was a health fair or a cultural event

    c. whenever they will be conducting a health fair or a cultural event

7. If teachers want to bring their students to see the store, _____ .

    a. when Penny's is welcoming them

    b. Penny's always welcomed them

    c. Penny's always welcomes them

2 Unscramble the sentences about company image. Add punctuation when necessary. Sometimes more than one answer is possible.

1. with the public / improve its image / acts responsibly / if / a company / it can

    If a company acts responsibly, it can improve its image with the public.

2. appreciate its actions / a socially responsible company / if customers / make a profit / is going to

    _____

3. choose to buy / if customers care / that company's products / about a company's social mission they might

    _____

4. if a company makes / an impact on the community / socially responsible decisions / it should have

    _____

5. may decide to donate money / if the organization's goals are related / a company / to an organization / to the company's product

    _____

6. is going to / the company's image / if consumers see instances / benefiting the community / of a company's policies / improve

    _____

7. an environmental or health problem / the company's public image / will be affected / if the company causes

    _____

8. will stay loyal / customers / keeps its promises / to a company / if the company

    _____

3 Complete the sentences about consumers' impact on companies. Write the word in parentheses in the correct blank. Capitalize the first word in each sentence.

1. _If_ people get _____ involved, _____ companies will make changes. (if)
   (a)   (b)   (c)

C 2. _____ companies will reduce negative effects _____ on the environment
   (a)   (b)

   _____ they use less energy. (if)
   (c)

C 3. When _____ more companies _____ think about corporate social
   (a)   (b)

   responsibility, consumers _____ have more choices. (will)
                              (c)

b 4. _____ companies _____ reduce their environmental footprint _____ if
   (a)   (b)   (c)

   they use solar energy. (can)

b 5. If _____ solar energy becomes more affordable, more companies _____ use it
   (a)   (b)

   _____ . (may)
   (c)

C 6. If _____ people show that they _____ care about their communities and the
   (a)   (b)

   environment, companies _____ respond. (should)
                           (c)

a 7. _____ people believe a company is socially responsible, _____ they are
   (a)   (b)

   _____ more likely to buy its products. (when)
   (c)

Present and Future Unreal Conditionals

1 Read the sentences about socially responsible companies. Then label each sentence *RC* (real conditional) or *UC* (unreal conditional).

1. _RC_ If a company wants to become socially responsible, it should be accountable to both its employees and the community.

2. _____ If a company were active in the community but not fair to its employees, it would not be a socially responsible company.

3. _____ For example, when a cereal company donates food to local hurricane victims, the company is acting responsibly.

4. _____ However, if the same company made its employees work unpaid overtime, it would not be acting responsibly.

5. _____ More companies might adopt socially responsible policies if their customers expected it.

6. _____ When a new business opens, the business owner may look around the community for ideas on getting involved.

7. _____ If a new small business opened in your community, what advice would you give the business owner on getting involved?

2 Read the sentences about volunteerism. Match the best word(s) to complete each sentence.

1. __e__ Many community organizations ____ out of business if they ____ volunteers.

2. ____ If no one volunteered, these organizations ____ people in need.

3. ____ It ____ more difficult to fill food banks if companies ____ food.

4. ____ Food banks could help more people if they ____ more donations.

5. ____ If community organizations ____ more widely in pursuit of donations, they might be able to get more volunteers.

6. ____ These organizations ____ very happy if they could get more volunteers with specialized skills.

7. ____ If people ____ the results of their donations, perhaps they ____ more often.

8. ____ If more people conducted a food drive or ____ , these organizations ____ even more good.

a. received

b. saw, would donate

c. volunteered, could do

d. would be

e. would go, didn't have

f. advertised

g. would be, didn't donate

h. couldn't help

3 Complete the present unreal conditionals about work in the community. Use the correct forms of the verbs in parentheses. Sometimes more than one answer is possible.

1. If our neighborhood _had_ more open space, we _would be able to_ have a community garden. (have, be able to)

2. If we _____ up the empty area at the end of the block, there _____ room for gardens for 20 families. (clean, be)

3. We _____ a lot of money if we _____ the work ourselves. (save, do)

4. If we _____ a corporate partner, maybe we _____ some donated equipment and materials. (have, get)

5. I wonder what the big hardware store in our neighborhood _____ if we _____ them for help. (say, ask)

6. It _____ good for their business if they _____ a local project. (be, sponsor)

7. If they _____ we were looking for donations, they probably _____ glad to help. (know, be)

8. If we _____ a partnership with the store, we probably _____ on other projects together in the future. (start, work)

4 Rewrite the following sentences. Use a present unreal conditional.

1. Brown Tree Industries is not a socially responsible company, and it doesn't make an effort to help the community.

   If Brown Tree Industries were a socially responsible company, it would make
   an effort to help the community.

2. The company doesn't donate money or time to community organizations, so it isn't a real member of the community.

   _____

3. The company's owner doesn't live in the community, so she isn't aware of some of the problems it has.

   _____

4. The owner doesn't know that schools in the area need donated school supplies, so her employees don't help collect them.

   _____

5. Since the owner isn't interested in acting responsibly, the company doesn't check all of its products to make sure they are safe.

   _____

6. Employees aren't encouraged to pay close attention to product safety, so the company's products don't have a good record with consumer organizations.

   _____

7. Because the company's employee policies aren't always fair, many community members won't buy its products.

   _____

8. Since a lot of community members don't buy the company's products, it isn't doing well.

   _____

5 Think about ways that you could be involved in your community. Write sentences that are true for you.

1. If I had more time, I would _____

   _____ .

2. If I knew how to _____ , I could

   _____ .

3. I would help _____ if

_____ .

4. If our community had _____ , I might

_____ .

Common Phrases with *Unless* and *If*

1 Complete the sentences about improving roadside conditions. Circle the correct words or phrases.

1. Our roads and highways would look much more attractive _____ throw trash on the sides of the road.

   (a.) if people didn't   b. if people don't   c. even if people

2. Roadsides can look terrible _____ they are kept clean.

   a. only   b. if not   c. unless

3. Cities and states can implement a volunteer Adopt-A-Road program _____ afford to hire workers to keep roads clean.

   a. unless they can't   b. if they can't   c. only if they can

4. Volunteers can have a big impact, _____ give a very small portion of their time.

   a. even if they   b. only if they   c. even they

5. Companies can give their employees time off to clean a section of a roadway, _____ getting a little dirty.

   a. if they don't mind   b. unless they don't mind   c. even if they don't mind.

6. _____ volunteered their labor, it would be a real shame.

   a. Only if   b. If no one   c. Even if

7. Children can volunteer to play a role in Adopt-A-Road programs, too, _____ are under 12 years of age.

   a. if not   b. if they only   c. unless they

8. _____ enough people volunteer can these programs stay strong and effective.

   a. Unless   b. Even if   c. Only if

2 Complete the article about social responsibility. Use the words in the box. You may use some words more than once.

even	if	not	only	no one	unless

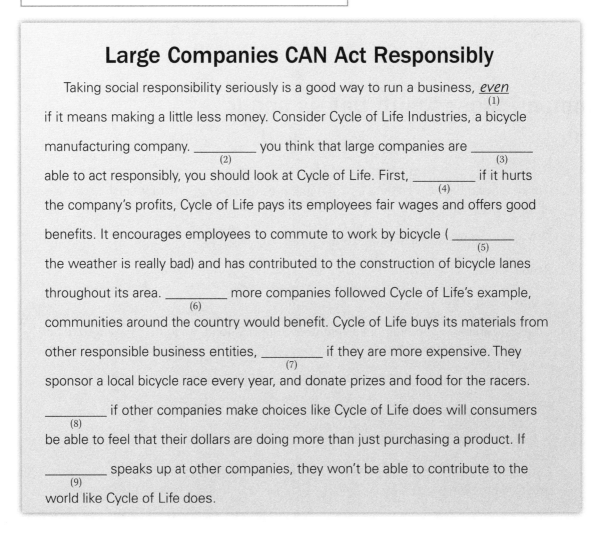

Large Companies CAN Act Responsibly

Taking social responsibility seriously is a good way to run a business, _even_ (1) if it means making a little less money. Consider Cycle of Life Industries, a bicycle manufacturing company. _____ (2) you think that large companies are _____ (3) able to act responsibly, you should look at Cycle of Life. First, _____ (4) if it hurts the company's profits, Cycle of Life pays its employees fair wages and offers good benefits. It encourages employees to commute to work by bicycle (_____ (5) the weather is really bad) and has contributed to the construction of bicycle lanes throughout its area. _____ (6) more companies followed Cycle of Life's example, communities around the country would benefit. Cycle of Life buys its materials from other responsible business entities, _____ (7) if they are more expensive. They sponsor a local bicycle race every year, and donate prizes and food for the racers.

_____ (8) if other companies make choices like Cycle of Life does will consumers be able to feel that their dollars are doing more than just purchasing a product. If _____ (9) speaks up at other companies, they won't be able to contribute to the world like Cycle of Life does.

3 Unscramble the sentences about volunteer vacations.

1. a volunteer vacation / if lying on the beach / you might enjoy / isn't the kind of vacation you like,

   If lying on the beach isn't the kind of vacation you
   like, you might enjoy a volunteer vacation.

2. part of your time working / volunteer vacations are a good way / even if you spend / to see a new place,

   _____

   _____

3. the evenings / working on construction or tutoring a child, / you'll have time to relax in / even if you spend the days

_____

4. are not too young / for families with children / volunteering is a great idea / if the children

_____

5. unless there are weather / sightseeing / or security concerns / volunteer vacations usually include

_____

6. more people go on volunteer vacations / only if / will conditions in communities around the world / improve

_____

7. will go on vacation / only if they don't have to / some people / do any work

_____

8. are one of them, / a volunteer vacation / unless you / you should consider

_____

Avoid Common Mistakes

1 Circle the mistakes.

1. (It won't be) possible for our company to "do good" **if** our CEO wasn't **concerned** about
   (a)   (b)   (c)
   helping the community.

2. A corporation might **being able to** increase its business **if** it **builds** public awareness
                       (a)   (b)   (c)
   of its policies.

3. **If** a company **make** an effort to focus on social responsibility, it can **make** a real
   (a)   (b)   (c)
   difference.

4. **If** Brown Tree Industries, **for instance**, required its employees to volunteer, it **can**
   (a)   (b)   (c)
   changed its image.

5. **Even** less socially responsible employees **will** **volunteer** if companies had a "culture
      (a)   (b)   (c)
   of volunteerism."

6. Companies might **work** to change public policy if they **thinks** it **will** improve
                    (a)   (b)   (c)
   their image.

7. **Only if** we all **refuse** to do business with anyone who uses child labor will the practice

(a)   (b)
finally **ends**.

(c)

8. Companies should **take** social responsibility seriously **otherwise** they **don't care** about

              (a)   (b)   (c)
the community.

2 Identify the common mistakes in the sentences. Label each sentence with the type of mistake from the box. If there is no mistake, write *e*. Then correct each sentence.

a. Remember that subjects and verbs in an *if* clause must agree.	c. Remember to use the correct form of the modal in real and unreal conditional sentences.
b. Remember that the base form of the verb follows a modal.	d. Do not confuse *otherwise* with *unless*.
	e. There is no mistake.

_c_ If a company really cares about its image, it ~~would~~ *will* a make an effort to let the

(1)
public know about its corporate policies. _____ For instance, a fast-food restaurant may

                                                     (2)
advertises its charitable activities on its napkins or coffee cups. _____ The company would

                                                    (3)
mention its environmental policies in its advertisements if it is proud of its work. _____ If a

                                                            (4)
company are not strong environmentally, it can choose to highlight its fair labor policies in
its public documents.

_____ When a company wants to become better known in the community, it should

(5)
consider sponsorships in its core areas. _____ If a company make products for children, it

                                                   (6)
might choose to sponsor a children's sports team or summer camp.

_____ If every company were socially responsible, communities might see some real

(7)
changes. _____ It's difficult to make those changes otherwise individuals play a role, too.

         (8)
_____ Real change can happen only if each person, and each organization, plays a part.

(9)

Self-Assessment

Circle the word or phrase that correctly completes each sentence.

1. If consumers want their money to have an effect, they _____ socially responsible products.

   a. looked for   b. were looking for   c. look for

2. Food banks could help more people if more restaurants _____ their unused food.

   a. donated   b. donate   c. are donating

3. Consumers _____ their opinion of a company if it begins to incorporate socially responsible policies.

   a. would change   b. changed   c. may change

4. Schools _____ students more effectively if more members of the community volunteered.

   a. might be able to help   b. are able to help   c. can help

5. Whenever _____ about a new green business or website, we always take a look at its products.

   a. we heard   b. we hear   c. we have heard

6. If I _____ a hybrid car, I would have a smaller environmental footprint.

   a. own   b. owned   c. owning

7. What area of business _____ if you wanted to open a green business?

   a. will you choose   b. you choose   c. would you choose

8. _____ green products are too expensive, people will usually buy them.

   a. When   b. Unless   c. If

9. Company managers may look for an activity to sponsor if they _____ about their company's public image.

   a. were concerned   b. are concerned   c. be concerned

10. Many companies allow their employees to volunteer on work time, _____ it means that they get less work done.

    a. if   b. only if   c. even if

11. _____ a garden, we would try to grow all of the vegetables our family needs.

    a. If we had   b. When we have   c. If we have

12. Change isn't always easy, so many people make changes _____ they see a good reason to.

    a. if   b. only if   c. unless

13. _____ everyone sees the importance of social responsibility, will the world be a better place.

    a. Only if   b. Even if   c. Unless

14. _____ I had a lot of money, I would be able to donate to charity.

    a. Even if   b. Unless   c. If

15. Even if I _____ much time, I try to do some work in the community.

    a. don't have   b. have   c. will have

Cause and Effect 4

Alternative Energy Sources

-ing Participle Phrases That Show Effect

1 Combine the sentences about alternative energy sources. Use an *-ing* participle that shows effect.

1. Solar-powered alternatives are an excellent choice. They save money and protect the environment simultaneously.

   Solar-powered alternatives are an excellent choice, *saving money and protecting the environment simultaneously*.

2. Many people now select solar-powered watches. They avoid the need to buy and recycle batteries.

   Many people now select solar-powered watches, _____ .

3. Smart international travelers use solar phone chargers. This makes it unnecessary to carry adapters and batteries.

   Smart international travelers use solar phone chargers, _____ .

4. Environmentally conscious householders cool their homes with solar-powered fans. They reduce their air-conditioning bills.

   Environmentally conscious householders cool their homes with solar-powered fans,

   _____ .

5. More and more people are investing in solar panels. They lower their energy costs.

   More and more people are investing in solar panels, _____ .

6. Some companies produce household appliances that can be charged with solar battery chargers. This decreases people's utility bills.

   Some companies produce household appliances that can be charged with solar battery

   chargers, _____ .

7. More homeowners are replacing objects that use electricity with those that use alternative power sources. This saves them money.

   More homeowners are replacing objects that use electricity with those that use

   alternative power sources, _____ .

2 Unscramble the sentences about biomass. Use the *-ing* form of the verbs in bold. Add commas when necessary.

1. sunlight and carbon dioxide / in photosynthesis / plants combine / **create** food

   In photosynthesis, plants combine sunlight and carbon dioxide, creating food.

2. to animals and people that eat them / **give** them energy / the chemical energy in plants / is passed on

   _____

3. **offer** us a good alternative to nonrenewable sources / there will always be / waste from animals and plants

   _____

4. **make** it a renewable resource / obtained from the waste of / plants and animals / is organic material / biomass

   _____

5. such as vegetable oil and animal fats / from leftover food products / **produce** biodiesel / energy is extracted

   _____

6. instead of oil / can be used / biomass / **make** the world / a better place

   _____

3 Complete each sentence with *thereby* and the *-ing* participle of the verb in parentheses.

1. The government offers tax credits to companies who use solar power and wind power,

   thereby decreasing costs for the consumer. (decrease)

2. Solar energy produces little noise, _____ the environment quieter and more

   peaceful. (make)

3. Wind energy uses the power of the wind, _____ electricity. (produce)

4. Some utility companies use solar power, _____ megawatts of electricity to

   thousands of homes. (supply)

5. Biomass fuels can be made from plant materials and animal waste, _____ an

   excellent source of renewable energy. (constitute)

6. Biomass provides building materials, paper, chemicals, and medicines, _____ us

   all. (benefit)

7. Wood waste and garbage can be burned to make electricity, _____ heat to homes

   and industries. (provide)

-ing Participle Phrases That Show Cause

1 Complete the sentences about geothermal energy. Use the -ing participle of the verb for the words in bold.

1. **Because it has** a lot of volcanoes, Iceland uses geothermal energy to provide some of its energy needs.

   Having a lot of volcanoes, Iceland uses geothermal energy to provide some of its energy needs.

2. **Because they live** in a country with a lot of geothermal energy, Icelanders get inexpensive heating for their homes.

   _____ in a country with a lot of geothermal energy, Icelanders get inexpensive heating for their homes.

3. **Because it comes** from deep inside the Earth, geothermal steam is very hot.

   _____ from deep inside the Earth, geothermal steam is very hot.

4. **Because it is** extremely hot when it comes from the Earth, geothermal steam must go through several processes to cool down.

   _____ extremely hot when it comes from the Earth, geothermal steam must go through several processes to cool down.

5. **Because it originates** from a nearby geothermal plant, the water of the Blue Lagoon is a pleasant temperature for bathing.

   _____ from a nearby geothermal plant, the water of the Blue Lagoon is a pleasant temperature for bathing.

6. **Because it contains** minerals such as calcium and magnesium, the water of the Blue Lagoon is believed to be healthy for the skin.

   _____ minerals such as calcium and magnesium, the water of the Blue Lagoon is believed to be healthy for the skin.

7. **Because it is located** near the capital of Iceland, the Blue Lagoon attracts many tourists.

   _____ near the capital of Iceland, the Blue Lagoon attracts many tourists.

8. **Because it heats** most of Iceland, including hotels, geothermal power intrigues many visitors to the country.

   _____ most of Iceland, including hotels, geothermal power intrigues many visitors to the country.

2 Complete the sentences with the correct forms of the verbs in parentheses. One of the verbs will be in -*ing* form.

1. *Providing* money for alternative energy projects, the government *supports* the development of renewable fuel production. (provide, support)

2. _____ a harmful effect on climate change, alternative sources of power such as solar, hydropower, and geothermal energy _____ the wave of the future. (not have, be)

3. _____ a possible cause of climate change, the consumption of fossil fuels _____ a controversial issue. (be, be)

4. _____ a healthier, safer environment, the government _____ sustainable energy sources such as wind and solar power. (want, invest in)

5. _____ weather and natural resources, alternative energy sources _____ better in some regions than others. (depend on, work)

6. For example, _____ only a few days of sunshine per year, cities in the Northwest _____ always the best places for solar energy. (have, not be)

7. On the other hand, _____ access to the Columbia River, Washington and Oregon _____ excellent locations for hydropower plants. (have, be)

8. In another example, _____ large amounts of geothermal resources, the Big Island of Hawaii _____ 30 percent of its power from geothermal energy. (possess, get)

3 Complete the sentences about your personal experiences. Write sentences that are true for you.

1. Coming from a large family, *I am rarely lonely* _____ .

2. Living in the United States, I _____ .

3. Speaking English, I _____ .

4. Having many friends, I _____ .

5. Having traveled to _____ (country or city),

   I _____ .

4 Match the phrases to correctly complete each sentence about energy sources.

1. _e_ Accounting for 16% of global electricity consumption,

2. ____ Standing 20 stories tall,

3. ____ In taking up to 630 gallons of water to prepare,

4. ____ Having 25 active volcanoes and many springs and geysers,

5. ____ By releasing hydrogen sulphide, a gas that smells like rotten eggs,

6. ____ Having been made from decomposed animals and plants million of years ago,

7. ____ Being one of the largest urban car-free zones in the world,

a. the city of Marrakesh has relatively low carbon emissions.

b. a typical hamburger uses a lot of natural resources.

c. Iceland heats many of its buildings using geothermal hot water.

d. the largest wind turbine in the world is in Hawaii.

e. water is the most widely used renewable energy source.

f. coal, petroleum, and natural gas are called "fossil" fuels.

g. geothermal energy creates some environmental concerns.

Verbs That Show Cause and Effect

1 Complete the sentences about fossil fuels. Circle the word or phrase that correctly completes each sentence.

1. The burning of fossil fuels such as coal and oil **(causes)** / **is caused by** air and water pollution.

2. Carbon dioxide **produces / is produced** when fossil fuels are burned.

3. The burning of fossil fuels **contributes to / is caused by** the greenhouse effect.

4. Climate change may **cause / be caused by** greenhouse gases.

5. The rise in global fossil fuel emissions **is caused by / contributes to** climate change.

6. Acid rain **produces / is produced** when fossil fuels are burned.

7. Acid rain **leads to / is caused by** slow growth and disease in forests.

8. The mining of coal, a very dangerous job, has **led to / been produced by** the deaths of thousands of miners.

9. In addition, a great deal of environmental damage **leads to / is caused by** coal mining.

10. Mining often **leads to / is produced by** deforestation – clearing and burning large areas of trees.

2 Complete the sentences on green (sustainable) buildings. Use the correct form of *result in* or *result from*.

1. Many benefits may _result from_ paying attention to how buildings are designed.

2. Interest in green building _____ the energy crisis of the 1970s.

3. One benefit is that green buildings can _____ lower energy costs.

4. Increased health and happiness can also _____ living and working in environmentally friendly buildings.

5. The interest in green building has _____ new types of architecture.

6. Growing plants on roofs and on the sides of green apartment buildings can _____ a closer connection to nature for the people who live in them.

7. Plants on rooftops can also _____ lower building temperatures, so residents use less air conditioning.

8. A smaller ecological footprint can _____ green building technologies.

9. The use of solar energy in green buildings may _____ fewer greenhouse emissions.

10. The use of sustainable woods such as bamboo in green building may also _____ saving trees.

3 Complete the paragraph about alternative fuels with *from*, *in*, or *to*.

Alternative **Fuels**

There are many reasons why we should use alternative fuels instead of fossil fuels.

One of the main reasons is that fossil fuels contribute _to_ climate change. Anything that
(1)

leads _____ climate change also results _____ dramatic effects on all life on
(2)   (3)

the planet. For example, warmer weather may result _____ climate change. This is
(4)

not all bad, as warmer weather might contribute _____ a longer growing season.
(5)

However, the shrinking of the glaciers may result _____ climate change. In addition,
(6)

warmer weather might result _____ larger populations of dangerous warm-weather
(7)

insects such as mosquitoes. Weather changes in general may also lead _____
(8)

drought and flood. This can contribute _____ serious problems with our food
(9)

supply, as drought and floods affect the growing of crops. Therefore, it is important that

we start thinking seriously about the types of energy sources we use.

Avoid Common Mistakes

1 Circle the mistakes.

1. Many negative **consequences** **result** (by) the use of fossil fuels.

(a)   (b)   (c)

2. **Burning** fossil fuels **results** **of** acid rain.

(a)   (b)   (c)

3. Studies **show** that wind power does not **contribute** **for** climate change.

(a)   (b)   (c)

4. The **use** of hybrid cars **contribute** **to** cleaner air.

(a)   (b)   (c)

5. An increased demand for energy has **resulted** **by** a dramatic **increase** in population.

(a)   (b)   (c)

6. **Increasing** demand may **result** **of** a complete lack of oil in the future.

(a)   (b)   (c)

7. Solar energy **contribute** **to** lower energy **costs** for homes and businesses.

(a)   (b)   (c)

8. Using alternative energy **sources** may **contribute** **for** improved air and water quality.

(a)   (b)   (c)

2 Identify the common mistakes in the sentences. Label each sentence with the type of mistake from the box. If there is no mistake, write *e*. Then correct each sentence.

---

a. Remember to use *result in*, not *result of*.	d. Remember that the subject and the verb must agree when using *contribute to*.
b. Remember to use *result from*, not *result by*.	
c. Remember to use *contribute to*, not *contribute for*.	e. There is no mistake.

>   *in*
> *a* The high cost of oil and other concerns have resulted ~~of~~ many people beginning to
>
(1)
> look at new energy sources. ____ They are interested in developing energy sources that
>
(2)
> contributes to a smaller environmental footprint. ____ An alternative energy source that
>
(3)
> has many advantages is solar power. ____ First, solar power does not contribute for air
>
(4)
> or water pollution. ____ For example, no emissions of any kind result by operating solar
>
(5)
> power plants. ____ Therefore, these plants do not contribute for climate change. ____ In
>
(6)   (7)
> addition, the production of solar energy results of no waste or garbage of any kind.

Self-Assessment

Circle the word or phrase that correctly completes each sentence.

1. ____ a windy area, central California is a good place for wind power.

   a. Be   b. Because   c. Being

2. _____ solar heating, green buildings do not have a negative impact on the environment.

   a. Using   b. Used   c. By

3. Buying local products reduces the need for transportation, _____ reducing pollution.

   a. thereby   b. but   c. causes

4. _____ using renewable energy sources, people can save money.

   a. Therefore   b. Thus   c. By

5. _____ learning about climate change, we have increased our interest in renewable energy.

   a. Causing   b. In   c. Thus

6. The world's population is growing, _____ causing an increase in demand for oil.

   a. thereby   b. by   c. in

7. _____ burning fossil fuels, we are contributing to climate change.

   a. Because of   b. Leading to   c. By

8. More electric cars on the road leads _____ less air pollution.

   a. to   b. from   c. in

9. Human activity is contributing _____ climate change.

   a. in   b. to   c. from

10. Acid rain results _____ damage to buildings and other structures.

    a. from   b. in   c. to

11. Some health problems _____ environmental pollution.

    a. cause   b. caused   c. are caused by

12. Lower building temperatures can _____ rooftop gardens.

    a. produce   b. be produced by   c. produces

13. Lower energy bills _____ the use of wind power in one California community.

    a. resulted in   b. resulted from   c. resulting

14. The use of wind power will contribute _____ a healthier environment.

    a. for   b. to   c. by

15. High gas prices result _____ people driving less.

    a. in   b. of   c. from

Identifying Relative Clauses

1 Read the sentences about good environments for children. Then label each sentence.

> S = subject relative clause
> O = object relative clause
> P = prepositional object relative clause

1. __S__ Parents **who create a stimulating environment** have children with fewer discipline problems.

2. _____ A study **that indicates these results** was published last fall.

3. _____ It is a study **with which many experts disagree**.

4. _____ In fact, a different study **that experts completed recently** shows opposite results.

5. _____ According to the first study, children **who live in a stimulating environment** are often more creative than other children.

6. _____ An environment **in which children can express their creativity** has many benefits.

7. _____ However, the over-stimulating environment **that some parents may provide** can be harmful for some children.

8. _____ In any case, parents **who are consistent** usually have better-behaved children.

2 Complete the sentences about birth order. Use the words in parentheses and add the correct relative pronoun. Sometimes more than one answer is possible.

1. Do children _who are born first_ tend to be driven? (the children are born first)

2. Are children _____ manipulative? (the children are born last)

3. These are ideas _____ about birth order. (many people have these ideas)

4. However, some birth order studies _____ in the last 40 years do not support these ideas. (researchers have done these studies)

5. Birth order research is a topic _____ . (many experts have strong ideas about this topic)

6. Some studies _____ support birth order characteristics like the ones described above. (these studies recently appeared in journals)

7. On the other hand, there are studies _____ for these personality characteristics. (the studies indicate completely different reasons)

8. For example, a study _____ showed the actual number of family members was more important than birth order. (the study looked at family size)

9. In that study, firstborn children who came from large families were more successful than firstborn children _____ . (the children came from small families)

3 Complete the sentences about caring for aging family members. Circle the correct pronouns to complete each sentence.

1. Aging parents **which** / **who** live near their children tend to feel happy and secure.

2. My aunt **which** / **who** lives with us has few worries.

3. Social workers **whose** / **that** work focuses mainly on the older generation can give good advice about aging relatives.

4. Some books and articles **who** / **that** have been published on this subject can also be very useful resources.

5. Some parents feel their children are the only people on **whom** / **which** they can rely.

6. Feeling vulnerable and scared are characteristics **whose** / **that** older people may display.

7. People **which** / **who** have very large extended families tend to feel more secure.

8. The research **that** / **whom** I just read helped me understand my grandparents better.

4 Complete the sentences about people and work. Write sentences that are true for you.

1. People whose work focuses on children *are very important to society* .

2. _____ are the people that I rely on most.

3. My friend who lives in (city or country) is _____ .

4. Work that involves _____ .

5. A brother or sister is someone who _____ .

5 Combine the sentences. Use a relative clause.

1. Some siblings fight as children. These siblings can have excellent relationships as adults.

   Some siblings *who fight as children can have excellent relationships as adults* .

2. Some people think sibling rivalry only affects young children. Those people should be aware it can also be a problem in adulthood.

   People _____ .

3. Many adult siblings have aging parents. Those siblings must sometimes cooperate in taking care of them.

   Adult siblings _____ .

4. One child may live closer to the parents. That child often has to spend the most time taking care of them.

   The child _____ .

5. Some parents have children that get along well as adults. Those parents tend to get the best care.

   Parents _____ .

6. Many older siblings are used to making decisions. They need to respect the views of their younger brothers and sisters.

   Older siblings _____ .

7. Some middle children act as peacemakers in families. These children may find conflict difficult.

   Middle children _____ .

Comparatives with *As . . . As*

1 Complete the web article with *as . . . as* structures. Use the adjectives and adverbs in parentheses.

Surprising Similarities

Identical twins Cristina and Isabel were raised in different families. They met for

the first time as adults. They were not very surprised by their physical similarities. For

example, Cristina was *as attractive as* (attractive) Isabel. She was _____
 (1)   (2)

(tall) her twin, as well. In addition, Cristina's hair was _____ (dark) Isabel's
                                                              (3)

hair. However, they were surprised by the similarities in their behavior. For example,

Isabel had cut her hair just _____ (recently) Cristina had, and her hair was
                               (4)

just _____ (short) her twin's. Also, Isabel spoke _____ (quickly)
      (5)   (6)

Cristina. When she spoke, she moved her hands _____ (energetically)
                                                  (7)

Cristina, too. They laughed in the same way, too. Each twin laughed _____
                                                                        (8)

(loudly) the other when someone told a joke.

---

2 Unscramble the sentences about Laura and Matt.

1. his twin Laura / Matt is not / as happy as

   Matt is not as happy as his twin Laura.

2. as he did / he is not doing as well / as a child

   _____

3. is not / as Laura's / as satisfying / Matt's life

   _____

4. Laura's / with his parents / Matt's relationship / is not as good as

   _____

5. as he was / Matt is not / when he was growing up / as secure now

   _____

6. as it was / as good now / when she was growing up / Laura's life is

   _____

7. as hard now / when she was in college / as she did / Laura works

_____

8. in her twenties / Laura is / as she was / when she was / as happy now

_____

3 Circle the words that best complete each sentence about the Rivera and Lee families.

1. The Riveras have four children. The Lees have five children.

   The Riveras do not have **as much** / **as many** children as the Lees.

2. Each Lee child does three hours of homework a night. Each Rivera child also does three hours of homework every night.

   The Lee children have **many** / **just as much** homework as the Rivera children.

3. The Lees have a dog, two cats, and a hamster. The Riveras have a bird and a rabbit.

   The Riveras don't have **quite as much** / **quite as many** pets as the Lees.

4. The Lee household is very noisy. By comparison, the Riveras are a quiet family.

   The Riveras are not **almost as** / **nearly as** noisy as the Lees.

5. The Rivera children take music lessons, do sports, and have volunteer jobs. The Lee children take music lessons and do sports.

   The Lee children are **not quite as** / **just as** busy as the Rivera children.

6. Mary Lee is 5 feet, 9 inches tall. Laura Rivera is 5 feet, 10 inches tall.

   Mary is **just as** / **nearly as** tall as Laura.

7. Amy Lee and Julie Rivera are in junior high. Amy plays four sports, but Julie plays only one.

   Julie is not **nearly as** / **quite** athletic as Amy.

4 Write sentences about your family that are true for you. Use each of the _as . . . as_ structures in the box.

is almost as	is just as	is nearly as	not nearly as	~~not quite as~~

1. _My sister is not quite as tall as me._____

2. _____

3. _____

4. _____

5. _____

Common Patterns That Show Contrast

1 Complete the sentences with the correct form of the prepositions in the box. You will use some words more than once.

between	from	in	to

1. Are there differences _between_ young children who stay at home and young children who go to day care?

2. Some studies show that children who go to day care tend to mature quickly. _____ contrast, children with stay-at-home mothers tend to mature more slowly.

3. A study on children's health showed a subtle difference _____ children who stay at home and children who go to day care.

4. The study showed that children who go to day care tend to get sick often. _____ contrast, children who stay at home are healthier.

5. Stay-at-home children often differ _____ day-care children in that they are more passive once they start school.

6. _____ contrast _____ stay-at-home children, some day-care children tend to exhibit more aggressive behavior once they start school.

7. Some day-care children differ _____ stay-at-home children in that they adapt more quickly to their environment once they start school.

8. However, most experts agree that the differences _____ day-care children and stay-at-home children are more often a feature of their personality, and not their preschool environment.

2 Circle the word or phrase that correctly completes each sentence.

The family is important in all cultures, but there are **differs /(differences)** between (1)

family types, even within the same culture. One major **differs / difference** is the role of (2)

work in the family. For some people, the needs of family members are more important

than work. **In contrast to / In contrast**, other people place work slightly above the (3)

needs of family members. The **differs / difference between** the values and priorities in (4)

the Green family and the Smith family is a good example of this. **In contrast / Unlike** (5)

the Green family's children, the children in the Smith family moved many miles away

from their parents for work. **In contrast / Unlike**, all the members of the Green family (6)

preferred to remain together in the same community; the children have stayed close to

home for their entire lives. The Green family also **differs from / different from** the Smith
family in that Mrs. Green did not work outside the home. **In contrast to / In contrast**
the Green family, the Smith children's mother worked outside the home. As a result, the
Smith children tended to **different from / differ from** the Green children in that they
were slightly more independent. Another **different from / difference between** the Green
family and the Smith family is that the Green family tended to have more contact with
members of their extended family. **Unlike / In contrast** the Smith family, many members
of the Green extended family lived near each other, in the same community.

3 Write five sentences comparing your family to another family. Use topics 1–5 listed below
and the contrast words and phrases in the box. Write sentences that are true for you.

difference(s) between	differ(s) from	in contrast,	in contrast to	unlike

1. family size
2. family rules
3. who works (mother, father, or both parents)

4. how far extended family members
   live from each other
5. who does chores

1. _Unlike my neighbor's family, all my family members live near each other._

2. _____

3. _____

4. _____

5. _____

Avoid Common Mistakes

1 Circle the mistakes.

1. The author **referred** to a study (who) **showed** new information on family size.
   (a)   (b)   (c)
2. Firstborn children do not have **the same** characteristics **than** children born later.
                              (a) (b)   (c)
3. Aging adults **who lives** with their children generally **have** better health.
              (a)   (b)   (c)
4. **Children receive** a lot of attention **tend** to **be** successful adults.
   (a)   (b)   (c)
5. Only children can have the **same** success **than** children **who** have siblings.
                               (a)   (b)   (c)
6. The majority of **experts study** birth order **do** not **agree** with Dr. Park's research.
                    (a)   (b)   (c)
7. A child **who have** an older and a younger sibling is not **as** likely to be creative.
          (a)   (b)   (c)
8. **In contrast**, some families provide an environment **who benefits** an only child.
   (a)   (b)   (c)

2 Identify the common mistakes in the sentences. Label each sentence with the type of mistake from the box. If there is no mistake, write *e*. Then correct each sentence.

> a. Do not use *who* with inanimate nouns.
> b. Do not omit the relative pronoun in subject relative clauses.
> c. Remember that the subject and the verb must agree in relative clauses.
> d. Use *the same as*, not *the same than*.
> e. There is no mistake.

<u>*b*</u> People have often thought of adopted children,
(1)   *who*
children ∧ are not raised by their biological parents, as

having social and emotional problems. _____ However,
(2)

a study who the Children's Health Research Center

published in 2008 shows that adopted children tend to

be happy and well adjusted. _____ The study indicated
(3)

several interesting facts about the characteristics

of children who are adopted. _____ It showed that a significant percentage of adopted
(4)

children who has siblings were adopted along with their brothers or sisters into the same

families. _____ Studies who look at the mental health of adopted children have looked
(5)

at children adopted with and without their siblings. _____ Most of these studies show
(6)

that children are adopted along with their siblings tend to be happier and healthier than

children who are not adopted with their siblings. _____ In addition, the study showed
(7)

that children who lives with adoptive parents tend to do well in school. _____ According
(8)

to parents who have both adopted and biological children, their adopted children have

the same levels of achievement in school than their biological children. _____ The study's
(9)

authors concluded that parents of adopted children tend to give their adopted children

the same degree of attention as their biological children. _____ Many experts agree that
(10)

this is one of the most important factors contribute to the health and welfare of children

in general.

Self-Assessment

Circle the word or phrase that correctly completes each sentence.

1. A person who _____ certain characteristics as a child does not necessarily have them as an adult.

   a. exhibiting   b. exhibits   c. exhibit

2. Children from large families do not always get _____ children from small families.

   a. as much attention as   b. as much attention   c. not as much attention as

3. A school environment _____ creativity is best for certain children.

   a. who encourages   b. encourages   c. that encourages

4. Benjamin Spock was _____ many parents relied on in the past.

   a. an author they   b. an author which   c. an author that

5. The doctor _____ wrote *Baby and Childcare* died in 1998.

   a. who   b. whose   c. which

6. It was a book _____ parents found useful advice on childrearing.

   a. that   b. in   c. in which

7. There were several popular experts on child care in the 1980s, but the author _____ wrote *Your Children and You* was the most widely read.

   a. who   b. what   c. in which

8. Children _____ are often less lonely than other children.

   a. whose are twins   b. which are twins,   c. who are twins

9. Adopted children tend to be as _____ non-adopted children.

   a. happy as   b. happy than   c. happily as

10. Mexican families tend to have more than one child. _____ Chinese families tend to have only one child.

    a. Unlike   b. In contrast to   c. In contrast,

11. School is sometimes not as easy for younger siblings _____ for older siblings.

    a. when it is   b. as it is   c. than it is

12. Parents today have _____ childrearing information as their parents did.

    a. as much   b. as many   c. nearly as

13. Older parents sometimes do not have _____ financial problems as younger parents.

    a. as much   b. as many   c. almost as

14. Both siblings get excellent grades, so the older child is _____ successful as the younger child.

    a. not nearly as   b. almost as   c. just as

15. In the past, American families differed _____ families in other cultures in that the children tended to leave home at an early age.

    a. from   b. than   c. to

Comparison and Contrast 2

Men, Women, and Equality

Complex Noun Phrases

1 Unscramble the noun phrases about Blanca's job to complete the sentences.

1. job / nine-to-five / traditional

   Blanca did not want a *traditional nine-to-five job* .

2. inequality / gender

   She was tired of _____ at her company.

3. entrepreneurs / successful / female

   She attended a conference on _____ .

4. training / business / hands-on

   The conference gave her some _____ .

5. owner / business / female

   Today, she is a _____ .

6. attractive / change / extremely / career

   It turned out to be an _____ .

7. schedule / work / flexible

   She has a _____ .

8. advantages / great / financial

   There are _____ , as well.

2 A Complete the sentences about female business owners. Use the words in the box.

between	expected	in	~~of~~	owning	who

1. A study looked at the styles *of* female business owners.

2. There are differences _____ male and female bosses.

3. Women _____ run businesses tend to allow flexible schedules.

4. Conditions _____ these organizations tend to be more favorable for employees.

5. They often give financial help to employees _____ to advance in the organization.

6. Women _____ businesses tend to be more highly educated than men who own businesses.

| for | of | that | wanting | with |

7. For example, there are more women _____ bachelor's degrees running businesses than men.

8. Women-owned businesses are often more attractive to employees _____ good benefits.

9. For example, the amount _____ vacation time that employees receive is higher in these organizations.

10. In addition, there are often more opportunities _____ advancement in these organizations.

11. Women-owned businesses tend to have environments _____ are cooperative, as well.

B Read the sentences in A again. Then answer the questions.

a. Which sentences in A have nouns modified by prepositional phrases? *1, 2, 4, 7, 9, 10*

b. Which sentences have nouns modified by relative clauses? _____

c. Which sentences have nouns modified by -*ing* phrases? _____

d. Which sentences have nouns modified by -*ed* phrases? _____

3 Unscramble the noun phrases to complete the sentences.

1. gender attitudes / a survey / financial matters / of / about

   Smith Investments recently conducted *a survey of gender attitudes about financial matters* .

2. in the survey / the men / women / who participated / and

   _____ had equal levels of education and similar incomes.

3. men and women / of / significant differences / emotional attitudes / in the

   The survey found _____ .

4. confidence / their financial futures / about / feelings of

   The majority of men in the survey tended to have _____ .

5. feelings / the future / positive / about

   In contrast, women did not tend to have _____ .

6. women / the study / the majority / in / of

   Men also tended to take financial risks, while _____ .
   were less likely to take risks with money.

7. money / in investment accounts / small amounts / of / growing

   The women who participated tended to have _____ .

8. money / larger amounts / of / much / invested

   In contrast, many of the men who responded tended to have accounts with

   _____ .

4 Complete the sentences about the Millennial Generation (people born between 1980 and
the mid-1990s). Use the words in parentheses to make noun phrases.

1. Society is beginning to recognize

   the contributions of the Millennial Generation to gender equality .
   (The Millennial Generation has made contributions to gender equality.)

2. _____ between Millennials and older generations is
   (A difference in gender roles is significant.)
   evident in their parenting styles.

3. _____ showed that many Millennials are not following
   (A study was released recently.)
   traditional parenting roles.

4. Millennials tend not to agree with _____ that mothers
   (The previous generation held a belief.)
   should stay home and take care of the children and that fathers should go to work.

5. _____ between Millennial men and previous
   (The difference is the most significant.)
   generations is their interest in the balance between work and family life.

6. _____ in the upbringing of their children is the cause
   (Millennial fathers' participation in this is increasing.)
   of this.

7. _____ is comforting.
   (This belief is popular.)

8. _____ is becoming more and more common for
   (Parenting is equal.)
   Millennial parents, creating a smaller gender gap at home.

Parallel Structure

1 Circle the best word or phrase to complete the sentences about American weddings. Use parallel structure.

1. American weddings have changed both in terms of etiquette and **stylish / stylishly /** **style**.

2. For example, they differ from the past because they tend to be less formal and **traditionally / less traditional / traditions**.

3. Traditionally, the bride's family had to pay for the wedding and **make all the arrangements / making all the arrangements / they made all the arrangements**.

4. They enjoyed – and sometimes dreaded – choosing the place for the wedding, sorting out the flowers and photography, and **to arrange for the food and drinks / arranged for the food and drinks / arranging for the food and drinks**.

5. Traditionally, it was the groom's family's responsibility to introduce themselves to the bride's family and **host a rehearsal dinner / hosting a rehearsal dinner / that they hosted a rehearsal dinner**.

6. Today, both the groom's and the bride's families may pay for the wedding and **making the plans for it / participate in the planning / participated in the planning**.

7. In the past, usually only a person's first wedding was large, expensive, and **formal / formally / was formal**.

8. Because remarriage is more accepted today than in the past, many people may have expensive first, second, and even **a third wedding / the third time they get married / third weddings**.

9. Today, some couples are choosing to have less expensive and **they are conscious of the environment / they have more environmentally conscious weddings / more environmentally conscious weddings**.

10. Modern weddings are often an expression of the couple's sense of style and **how they approach life / they approach life / approach to life**.

2 Complete the sentences. Use the words in parentheses to make parallel structure. Sometimes more than one answer is possible.

1. The purpose of marriage in ancient China was to have children and

   <u>to create a partnership between two families</u>.
   (They wanted to create a partnership between two families.)

2. The first step in a traditional marriage in ancient China was the

   proposal and _____ .
   (Accepting the proposal was part of the first step.)

3. An important part of the pre-wedding phase was gift giving and

   _____ .
   (Choosing the date for the wedding was an important part of the pre-wedding phase.)

4. The groom's family gave the bride's family money and tea, while

   _____ .
   (The bride's family's gifts to the groom's family were food and clothing.)

5. A matchmaker helped the groom's family find a bride, presented the proposal to the bride's

   family, and _____ .
   (A matchmaker carried the gifts back and forth between the two families.)

6. Before the wedding, the bride moved away from her parents' house and

   _____ .
   (The bride lived with friends.)

7. An older married couple bought the bride and groom a bed and

   _____ .
   (The older couple covered it with special fruits.)

8. These fruits symbolized the desire for wealth and _____ .
   (They hoped for many children.)

9. Because there was music and fireworks, the start of the wedding was joyful and

   _____ .
   (There was a lot of noise.)

10. Both the bride and the groom wore red for good luck and _____ .
    (They wanted to be happy.)

11. During the ceremony, the groom would bow to show respect for the gods, for his bride, and

    _____ .
    (He would show respect for his parents.)

3 Write sentences about weddings in your culture. Use parallel structure in your answers.

1. What are three things a bride or groom in your culture must do before or during a wedding?

   <u>In my culture, a bride and groom must choose a wedding date, send</u>

   <u>invitations to friends and relatives, and buy rings before the wedding.</u>

2. What are three adjectives that describe a traditional wedding in your culture?

   _____

3. What are three types of people who are invited to a wedding in your culture?

   _____

Common Quantifiers

1 Complete the sentences about a class survey. Circle the best quantifier in parentheses for the words in bold.

1. I conducted a survey of my classmates on parenting roles. **Three** of my 20 questions asked for personal information such as age. (**A few**/ **Almost all**)

2. However, **17** of the questions focused on the roles that their parents had in the family when they were growing up. (**most / all**)

3. I was lucky because **0 percent** of the students were absent that day. (**no / none**)

4. In fact, **100 percent** of my classmates participated in the survey. (**most / all**)

5. **Ninety-five percent** of the students grew up with working mothers. (**Almost all / Several**)

6. Only **5 percent** of my classmates grew up with stay-at-home mothers. (**a little / a few**)

7. **Thirty percent** of the students said their fathers helped with the housework. (**Most / Some**)

8. **Seventy-five percent** of the students said that their mothers and their fathers shared the child care. (**Most / All**)

9. **Many** of my classmates said that they grew up with stay-at-home fathers. (**a great many / both**)

2 Complete the sentences about the 2006 Census. Use the correct quantifier.

~~many~~	much

According to the 2006 Census, there were _many_ stay-at-home fathers in the United
                                          (1)
States – approximately 159,000. However, there is not _____ research on men who
                                                        (2)
choose to raise their children instead of going to work every day.

no	most of

There are two categories of stay-at-home fathers: those who earn an income and those

who don't. _____ the fathers take care of their children but still have some income.
            (3)
The rest of the fathers do not work at all and have _____ income of their own.
                                                     (4)

> | little   a few |

Researchers have been studying stay-at-home mothers for some time now. As a result, there are _____ reliable studies on the mental health of women who stay at home
              (5)

to raise their children. However, there is _____ information on the mental health of
                                       (6)

fathers who do this.

> | a great many   a few |

In one study, only _____ stay-at-home fathers – about 5 percent – reported
                   (7)

feelings of depression. In fact, _____ of the respondents reported feelings of
                              (8)

satisfaction with their choices.

3 Complete the paraphrased sentences about working and responsibilities at home. Circle the correct adverb + comparative quantifier combination to complete each sentence.

1. "Both my parents worked full-time, but my mom did most of the housework and the cooking. My dad did little work around the house."

   The speaker's mother did **slightly more** / (**significantly more**) housework than her father.

2. "When I get married, I'll probably expect my husband to do at least a little more housework than my dad did."

   The speaker expects her husband to do **considerably more / slightly more** housework than her father did.

3. "My mother had almost all of the child-care responsibility. My father did only a little child care."

   The speaker's father did **substantially more / substantially less** child care than her mother did.

4. "My father had every weekend free, but my mother had to take care of us on the weekends. She really didn't have much free time."

   The speaker's mother probably had **slightly less / considerably less** free time than his father did.

5. "My dad did a great deal of the child care because he worked at home. Few of the children at my school had stay-at-home dads, and none of them in my neighborhood did."

   It is likely that **significantly fewer / considerably more** children in the speaker's school had stay-at-home fathers than stay-at-home mothers.

6. "My dad did most of the cooking, I guess because he was home more. My mom did some of the cooking, but she mostly cooked on the weekends."

   The speaker's mother did **slightly more / considerably less** cooking than her father did.

7. "Both my mother and my father worked full-time. We didn't see them for much of the time – they both worked so hard. But we lived with my grandmother and grandfather."

   The speaker spent **considerably more / considerably less** time with his grandparents than with his parents when he was growing up.

8. "My grandfather did housework and took care of us, even though he was from another generation. He was also from a culture where men did not do any housework or child care."

   The speaker's grandfather was **slightly less / substantially more** involved in raising children than other men from his cultural background.

Avoid Common Mistakes

1 Circle the mistakes.

1. There are more men in **professions** such as **nursing** and (to be teachers).
   (a)   (b)   (c)

2. The boys enjoyed **playing** sports and **to pretend to be** **soldiers**.
   (a)   (b)   (c)

3. The girls did not tend **to fight** or **wrestling** during **recess**.
   (a)   (b)   (c)

4. The boys **preferred** games that were **competitive** and **to be active**.
   (a)   (b)   (c)

5. The girls preferred activities that were **cooperative** and **being less active** **during** PE.
   (a)   (b)   (c)

6. Some parents feel that they should **give** masculine toys to their daughters and **to**
   (a)   (b)
   encourage them **to participate** in sports.
                    (c)

7. Most parents hope that their children will be able **to do** what they want in life and
   (a)
   not suffering from **gender discrimination**.
   (b)   (c)

8. Most schools tend to create a gender-neutral environment for children and **providing**
   (a)
   opportunities for them **to express** themselves.
   (b)   (c)

2 Identify the common mistakes in the sentences. Label each sentence with the type of mistake from the box. If there is no mistake, write *e*. Then correct each sentence.

> a. Remember to use parallel structure with two or more adjectives.
> b. Remember to use parallel structure with two or more noun phrases.
> c. Remember to use parallel structure with two or more verb phrases.
> d. Remember to use parallel structure with two or more clauses.
> e. There is no mistake.

_b_ Title IX, a law that was passed in 1972, requires equality in
(1)
education for males and ~~it also requires it for~~ females. _____ As the law
(2)
states: "No person in the United States shall, on the basis of sex, be
excluded from participation in, be denied the benefits of, or you cannot subject them
to discrimination under any education program or activity receiving Federal financial
assistance." _____ Title IX applies to any educational program that receives federal funding,
(3)
including public institutions of higher education such as colleges and universities, and
to vocational schools and it also applies to professional schools. _____ Two significant
(4)
benefits of Title IX are the rise in women's participation in athletics and the enrollment of
women in institutions of higher education has increased, too. _____ Before Title IX, there
(5)
were few opportunities for girls who wanted to play on school teams or participate in
school-sponsored athletic activities. _____ Today, thanks to Title IX, women play on
(6)
college sports teams, female athletes receive sports scholarships, and the rising popularity
of women's sports. _____ Because of the access to sports and higher education that Title
(7)
IX affords, many women now lead lives that are healthier, happier, and they receive more
rewards.

Self-Assessment

Circle the word or phrase that correctly completes each sentence.

1. There was a _____ between the salaries of men and women in the past.

   a. differ significantly   b. significant difference   c. different significance

2. A large percentage _____ college graduates are women.

   a. of   b. who   c. in

3. Many women _____ business degrees are working at major corporations.

   a. with   b. in   c. of

4. _____ to gender equality is significant.

   a. The study contribution   b. The contribution of the study   c. The study contributed

5. _____ are experiencing gender equality.

   a. College students were   b. Recently hiring   c. Recently hired
      recently hired   college students   college graduates

6. A study found that female bosses tend to be fair, generous, and _____ .

   a. cooperative   b. cooperation   c. they cooperate

7. Some studies show that marriage benefits men more than _____ .

   a. the benefit of women   b. women benefit   c. women

8. The school tries to treat children fairly and _____ the same opportunities to both girls and boys.

   a. they give   b. giving   c. give

9. Women who participate in college sports tend to be happy and _____ later on in life.

   a. they are successful   b. successful   c. succeed

10. In the past, some women experienced discrimination when they applied to college or _____ for a raise.

   a. when they asked   b. asking   c. to ask

11. _____ women experience discrimination in athletics nowadays.

   a. Few   b. A little   c. Little

12. In the past, women did not expect their husbands to do _____ child care.

   a. much   b. many   c. as the same

13. There is _____ information about salary differences between men and women.

   a. several   b. a great deal of   c. a great many

14. Only 5 percent of female students do not plan on working. In fact, _____ women expect to work.

   a. slightly more   b. considerably fewer   c. considerably more

15. There are ten male managers and nine female managers at JP Corporation. There are _____ female managers than male managers.

   a. slightly fewer   b. considerably fewer   c. significantly less

Comparison and Contrast 3

Family Values in Different Cultures

Comparative and Superlative Adjectives and Adverbs

1 Complete the sentences about immigrant families in the United States. Use the correct comparative or superlative form of the word in parentheses. Add *than* where needed.

1. *The largest* number of immigrant families come to the United States from Latin American and Asian countries. (large)

2. There are many differences among families of a single culture. Therefore, the families of a particular culture can be _____ many people realize. (diverse)

3. Determining the truth about how close family members are can be _____ determining their perceptions about it. (hard)

4. Of all members of a society, recent immigrants are _____ to discuss their family situations because they are not comfortable with revealing too much personal information. (likely)

5. As people age, they tend to view the family as _____ aspect of their lives. (important)

6. In many cultures, families with many children are considered _____ families with fewer children. (lucky)

7. One immigrant from Latin America said, "My grandparents work _____ I do at preserving our home culture." This is true for many immigrant families. (hard)

8. Living with a different family is often accepted in immigrant communities _____ in non-immigrant communities because living with people of the same culture is important. (readily)

9. Above all other factors, many immigrants rated financial security as _____ factor when choosing to live with non-relatives. Comfort with culture is also rated highly. (significant)

2 Complete the paragraph about different perspectives on family values. Use the words in the box or Ø. You will use some words more than once.

less	more	than	as
than	the least	the most	

A major American university surveyed its students about their opinions on family

values across cultures. The survey only focused on students between the ages of 18 and 21

who had lived in the United States longer _than_ 10 years. The results showed that Latino
(1)

and Asian families were perceived to be _____ oriented toward family than families
(2)

of European descent, who tended to place less value on families. Although Latino families

were perceived as _____ devoted of the groups in the study, the Latino results were
(3)

only slightly higher than those for Asian families. In addition, Middle Eastern families

were also perceived to be closer _____ European families, but not _____ close
(4) (5)

as Latino and Asian families. A majority of students reported that families of European

background were more individualistic _____ because in these cultures, the group
(6)

is _____ important than individual members. Similarly, students believed families
(7)

of European ancestry were _____ likely of all to have three generations of family
(8)

members living together. In fact, only 5 percent of students believed this would be likely.

3 Complete Roberto's blog about customs for formal and informal gatherings in different
cultures. Match the best words to complete each sentence.

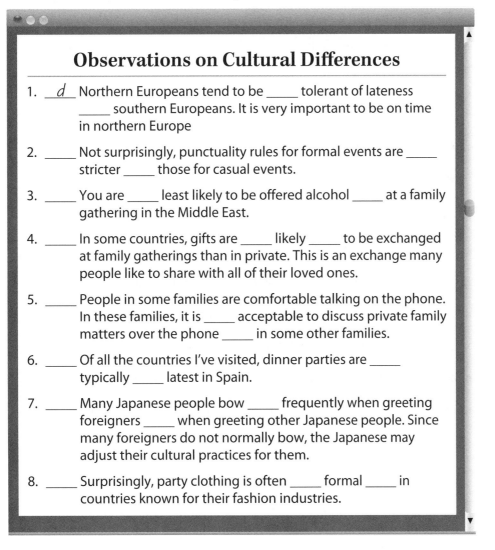

Observations on Cultural Differences

1. __d__ Northern Europeans tend to be _____ tolerant of lateness
_____ southern Europeans. It is very important to be on time
in northern Europe

2. _____ Not surprisingly, punctuality rules for formal events are _____
stricter _____ those for casual events.

3. _____ You are _____ least likely to be offered alcohol _____ at a family
gathering in the Middle East.

4. _____ In some countries, gifts are _____ likely _____ to be exchanged
at family gatherings than in private. This is an exchange many
people like to share with all of their loved ones.

5. _____ People in some families are comfortable talking on the phone.
In these families, it is _____ acceptable to discuss private family
matters over the phone _____ in some other families.

6. _____ Of all the countries I've visited, dinner parties are _____
typically _____ latest in Spain.

7. _____ Many Japanese people bow _____ frequently when greeting
foreigners _____ when greeting other Japanese people. Since
many foreigners do not normally bow, the Japanese may
adjust their cultural practices for them.

8. _____ Surprisingly, party clothing is often _____ formal _____ in
countries known for their fashion industries.

a. less / Ø

b. less / than

c. more / than

d̸. less / than

e. Ø / than

f. more / Ø

g. the / Ø

h. Ø / the

Articles

1 Complete Sandra's notes for her project on marriage customs in different cultures. Use the correct indefinite article (*a/an*) or Ø if no article is needed.

1. In many cultures, a woman older than 30 may have _a_ difficult time finding a suitable husband.
2. In some cultures, it is not uncommon for _____ girls under 18 to be married and have _____ children.
3. In many Middle Eastern cultures, _____ young married men often live in _____ apartment with their parents as well as their wife and children.
4. Sometimes _____ newly married couple's parents give them _____ appliances for their home, such as _____ washing machine and _____ dryer.
5. In the United States, people may marry even if _____ money is tight, but in some cultures, _____ couples might not marry unless they have _____ financial security.
6. In the United States, it is not uncommon for _____ urban families to live first in _____ apartment. They may later move to _____ duplex when their children are older.
7. It can be difficult to adjust to living with _____ new people or in _____ new place.
8. In some cultures, most families live in _____ apartments, and it is common for _____ older relatives to live with them.

2 Complete Lisa's personal web page about her memories of Barranquilla, Colombia. Use the correct indefinite or definite article (*a/an* or *the*) or Ø.

When I was _a_ child, my family and I lived in Colombia, _____ country near
                (1)   (2)
Venezuela. We lived in _____ city called Barranquilla. Barranquilla has always been _____
                        (3)   (4)
diverse city, and it has attracted many of Colombia's recent immigrants. As a result,

Barranquilla is _____ Colombian city with _____ most international flavor. There are
                 (5)   (6)
many ethnic groups, and each used to live in _____ area that had _____ special shops
                                              (7)   (8)
and restaurants. These shops and restaurants reflected _____ culture and taste of that
                                                        (9)
specific ethnic group. Over time, there has been _____ lot of intermarrying, so you can
                                                  (10)
easily find _____ people of Lebanese, Spanish, Italian, and German descent.
             (11)

3 Complete Bree's e-mail to her family in Canada. Use the correct articles (*a/an* or *the*) or Ø.

---

send

to Mom and Dad

cc

subject My classes in *the* U.S.
                   (1)

I | **B** | <u>U</u> | T▾ | T<small>T</small>▾

Hi Mom and Dad,

    I wanted to tell you a little about what I am learning from my classmates in my classes that started this week. Tim and Erica are ＿＿＿ sociology
(2)
classmates of mine. They are brother and sister; they are ＿＿＿ twins. Their
(3)
mother is from Morocco, and their father is from ＿＿＿ country in Asia, I can't
(4)
remember which. He works for ＿＿＿ UN. I enjoy their contributions to class
(5)
discussions because I always gain ＿＿＿ bit of insight into different cultures.
(6)
Because of them, I now have ＿＿＿ idea about ＿＿＿ role of the extended
(7)   (8)
family in Moroccan culture as well as ＿＿＿ way in which older people are
(9)
treated in Moroccan culture. It's been ＿＿＿ interesting class this semester. In
(10)
fact, it has been ＿＿＿ most interesting class all year!
(11)
    I don't have much time to write this e-mail, so I will write more tomorrow after class. I miss you, and I can't wait for you to visit me in October!

Love,

Bree

Common Expressions That Show Similarity

1 Complete the sentences about the similarities between Japanese and Chinese culture. Write the words in parentheses in the correct blank. Capitalize the first word in each sentence.

1. Some cultures, such as those of China and Japan, may appear different at first, but

   _____ in reality they _____ may have a lot *in common* . (in common)
   (a)   (b)   (c)

2. For example, the Chinese and Japanese written languages _____ are
                                                              (a)

   _____ each other because Japan's writing system is _____ partly
   (b)   (c)

   based on Chinese characters. (similar to)

3. Buddhism has been one part of Chinese culture for centuries _____ .
                                                                 (a)

   _____ , Buddhism has also had a role in Japanese _____
   (b)   (c)

   history. (likewise)

4. _____ , Confucianism has also played _____ a strong role in
   (a)   (b)

   _____ Japanese and Chinese cultures. (similarly)
   (c)

5. _____ China, Japan has a long tradition of martial arts. Major forms of
   (a)

   _____ martial arts were developed and are practiced in both _____
   (b)   (c)

   countries. (like)

6. The two countries have _____ : the Chinese had to defend against _____
                            (a)   (b)

   Mongol invaders from the north, _____ and so did the Japanese. (a lot in common)
                                     (c)

7. Some scholars believe that these early shared _____ experiences are the reason
                                                   (a)

   why _____ there are meaningful _____ between the two cultures
        (b)   (c)

   today. (similarities)

2 Complete the paragraph about special birthday celebrations in Latin America. Use the words in the box.

have something	likewise	like
similar to	~~similarities~~	in common

The Quinceañera is the celebration of a girl's

15th birthday in many Latin American cultures.

The traditions differ from country to country, but

the *similarities* between one country and another
    (1)

are quite striking. For example, regardless of country, the celebrations begin in the same

way. In Argentina and Mexico, the celebration begins with a waltz. _____ ,
                                                                          (2)

in Venezuela, Colombia, and Ecuador, the celebration also begins with a waltz. These

three countries have another thing _____ : a dance called the Paso Doble.
                                          (3)

_____ the dances, the dresses of Quinceañera celebrations _____
       (4)   (5)

in common. For example, Nicaragua is _____ Mexico in that girls traditionally
                                              (6)

wear pink. Pastel colors and white are also becoming more popular.

Avoid Common Mistakes

1 Circle the mistakes.

1. It took **longer** than I expected to finish my paper on the **most** important aspects of (The)
        (a)   (b)   (c)
   Dr. Spock's cultural research.

2. One culture is not **more better** than another. No culture is **the** same as another.
                        (a)   (b)   (c)

3. It is **more** likely that one family's beliefs are not **Ø** same as **another's**.
          (a)   (b)   (c)

4. Experts say that no one culture is more **friendlier** than another. However,
                                            (a)

   one culture's value of friendliness might not be **the** same **as** another's.
                                                     (b)   (c)

5. In some cultures, having a lot of children is **more desirable** than in others, but
                                                  (a)   (b)

   according to **the** Professor Silvia Luz, there are many differences within a culture.
                  (c)

6. My values are not **the** same as my friend's; he is **more** closer to his family and **more**
                       (a)   (b)   (c)

   interested in spending time with them.

7. I go to the **best** doctor, and although she trained overseas, her accent is not **more**
                  (a)   (b)

   harder to understand than many others.
     (c)

8. My **most** childhood memories are of spending time on my grandfather's farm in Mexico;
         (a)

   I wish I could have stayed there **Ø longer**.
                                      (b)   (c)

2 Identify the common mistakes in the sentences. Label each sentence with the type of mistake from the box. If there is no mistake, write *e*. Then correct each sentence.

> a. Remember to use *more* or *-er* in comparisons. Do not use both.
> b. Remember to use *best*, not *most*, before nouns.
> c. Do not use the definite article *the* with title/position + name.
> d. Remember to use *the* in the expression *the same as*.
> e. There is no mistake.

  a In recent years, some universities have made a ~~more~~ bigger effort to make their
  (1)
international students feel welcome on campus. Several universities have a campus

activities director who is responsible for planning outings for international students. The

director at this university is Josh Brown. _____ The Mr. Brown has been an instructor of
                                          (2)
English here for three years, _____ and now he is having a larger role in his students' lives
                              (3)
by coordinating their social events. _____ Of course the interests of one group of students
                                     (4)
are never same as another, so it is important to offer different activities each semester.

_____ Last semester, one of the most-reviewed activities was a trip to Niagara Falls.
 (5)
However, this semester, only a handful of students took the trip. _____ This shows that the
                                                                  (6)
most-planned programs are not always successful. _____ In order to offer more variety,
                                                  (7)
Mr. Brown is going to plan a new program. _____ He hopes to have a more wider range of
                                          (8)
activities, including activities to learn about American sports, food, and holidays.

Self-Assessment

Circle the word, phrase, or item that correctly completes each sentence.

1. Some people find cultural discussions to be _____ interesting than others do.

   a. Ø   b. more   c. the most

2. To understand the difficulties of living in _____ new culture, we can speak to new immigrants.

   a. a   b. the   c. Ø

3. _____ France and Spain, Italy is a major tourist destination.

   a. Similarly   b. Like   c. Likewise

4. Learning about other cultures was _____ enjoyable part of my international relations class.

   a. Ø   b. more   c. the most

5. Some immigrants _____ embrace the customs of a new culture than others do.

   a. more ready   b. most ready   c. more readily

6. Asian and Latino cultures are different, but one thing they have _____ is their respect for age.

   a. likewise   b. similarly   c. in common

7. Of all the countries I've lived in, I had _____ difficult time adapting to Brazilian culture.

   a. Ø   b. less   c. the least

8. To feel comfortable in a new country, most people try to learn the language of _____ country.

   a. a   b. the   c. Ø

9. Essentially, the role of women in Canadian society is _____ the role of women in the United States.

   a. in common   b. similar to   c. similarities

10. It is impossible to say that one culture is _____ better than another.

    a. Ø   b. more   c. the most

11. The value of _____ money varies from culture to culture and from family to family.

    a. a   b. the   c. Ø

12. The headquarters of _____ UN are in New York.

    a. a   b. Ø   c. the

13. The headquarters of _____ NATO are in Brussels, Belgium.

    a. a   b. the   c. Ø

14. For some immigrants, preserving their culture may be _____ important than integrating.

    a. Ø   b. more   c. the most

15. Many poor families view education as necessary. _____ , many wealthy families want their children to get a good education.

    a. Likewise   b. Similar to   c. Like

Comparison and Contrast 4

Intercultural Communication

Adverb Clauses of Contrast and Concession

1 Read the sentences about appropriate behavior in international business meetings. Then label the words in bold in each sentence.

> CT = clause of contrast   CN = clause of concession

1. _CT_ The exchange of business cards is highly ceremonial in Japan, **while in the United States it is more casual**.

2. _____ **Although it may be difficult to identify the most senior person at the meeting**, it is important that negotiators give their business cards to him or her first.

3. _____ Some businesspeople may exchange business cards **even though they may not necessarily do business in the future**.

4. _____ Shaking hands at the beginning of a business meeting is common in the United States, **whereas bowing is more common in East Asia**.

5. _____ In East Asia, senior executives will bow to junior executives, **although the bow will not be as deep**.

6. _____ **While negotiating a contract in the United States with junior executives is often acceptable**, it may be more appropriate to negotiate with the most senior executive in other cultures.

7. _____ Many employees stay late to work in some regions like New York City, **whereas leaving work on time is required in other parts of the world**.

8. _____ **Though executives may try to end a meeting on time**, unavoidable delays can arise.

9. _____ Depending on company policy, meetings in the United States these days can be informal, **while in the past they invariably used to be formal**.

10. _____ **Whereas many companies in the U.S. pay their employees overtime,** others expect their employees to work extra hours without pay.

2 Complete the web article about international business practices. Match the phrases to correctly complete each sentence.

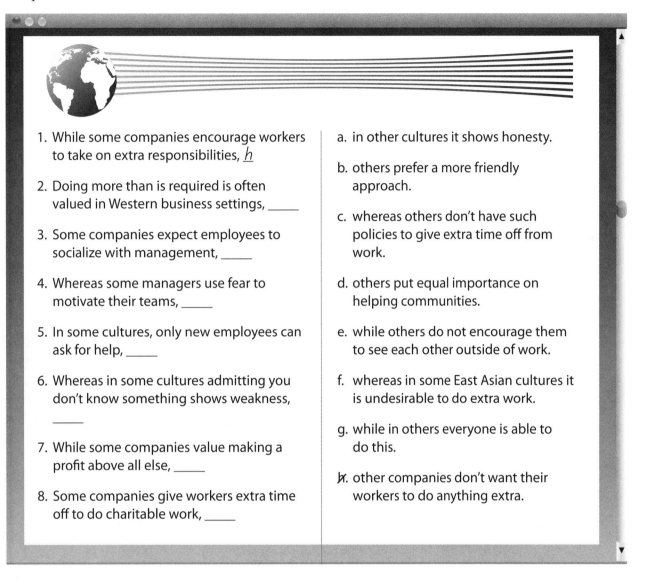

1. While some companies encourage workers to take on extra responsibilities, _h_

2. Doing more than is required is often valued in Western business settings, _____

3. Some companies expect employees to socialize with management, _____

4. Whereas some managers use fear to motivate their teams, _____

5. In some cultures, only new employees can ask for help, _____

6. Whereas in some cultures admitting you don't know something shows weakness, _____

7. While some companies value making a profit above all else, _____

8. Some companies give workers extra time off to do charitable work, _____

a. in other cultures it shows honesty.

b. others prefer a more friendly approach.

c. whereas others don't have such policies to give extra time off from work.

d. others put equal importance on helping communities.

e. while others do not encourage them to see each other outside of work.

f. whereas in some East Asian cultures it is undesirable to do extra work.

g. while in others everyone is able to do this.

h. other companies don't want their workers to do anything extra.

3 Complete the sentences about the differences between business e-mails in the United States and the United Kingdom. Use *although*, *though*, *while*, *whereas*, or Ø. Sometimes more than one answer is possible.

1. _Although/Though_ e-mail is used in business communication all over the world, the style of e-mail language varies from country to country.

2. Although English is the official language of the United Kingdom and the United States, _____ the language and style of business e-mails is quite different.

3. _____ a company may have an office in the United Kingdom and the United States, the e-mail styles may be different.

4. _____ Americans often omit greetings in their business e-mails, it is considered somewhat rude to do this in the United Kingdom.

5. Many British e-mails begin with "Dear" followed by the person's name, _____ American e-mails frequently begin with the name only.

6. Businesspeople in the U.K. may often include pleasantries in e-mails, _____ Americans may not include them in the reply.

7. _____ the e-mail style of the United States strives for clarity, but it may be considered abrupt.

8. _____ Americans tend not to include many pleasantries in e-mails, they tend to use pleasantries when conducting business over the phone.

9. Although there are differences in styles, _____ communication is usually successful.

Transition Words and Phrases That Show Contrast and Concession

1 Rewrite the sentences about clothing in different cultures. Use the words in parentheses.

1. Many Asian women wear fashionable clothing at social gatherings, but business attire is far more conservative. (nonetheless)

   Many Asian women wear fashionable clothing at social gatherings; nonetheless, business attire is far more conservative.

2. Businessmen's clothing doesn't change dramatically across cultures, but businesswomen's clothing does. (on the other hand)

   _____

3. Informal clothing is acceptable in the United States, but it may not be suitable in other countries. (in contrast)

   _____

4. While trying to look professional, American women may find that their clothing is not appropriate in all international business environments. (in spite of)

   _____

5. Latin American and European women can wear colorful business clothing in their own countries, but they should wear neutral colors when doing business in East Asia and the Middle East. (nevertheless)

   _____

6. Pant suits for women are accepted in the United States, but they are not always accepted in Japan and the Middle East. (conversely)

_____

7. Businesswomen can show their knees in the United States, but they should not do this in Russia, India, or East Asia. (however)

_____

8. Businesswomen in Russia, India, or East Asia might wear more conservative clothing, not skirts. (instead of)

_____

2 Complete Jessica's blog post about gift-giving customs around the world. Circle the transition word or phrase that correctly completes each sentence.

1. In Latin American countries, gifts can be given at the beginning of a meeting. **Instead of /** **In contrast**/ **Despite**, it is appropriate to give a gift at the end of the meeting in Asia and the Middle East.

2. Personal clothing is never a good idea for a business gift; **however / despite / in spite of**, if you have known the person for a long time, you may be able to bend this rule.

3. American businesspeople do not typically exchange expensive gifts with each other; **nevertheless / instead of / despite**, they will exchange inexpensive gifts such as notebooks and pens.

4. Gifts with company logos are appropriate in China. **Conversely / In spite of / Despite**, such gifts are inappropriate in Japan.

5. Expensive gifts are prized in Korea. In Canada, **despite / instead / on the other hand**, gifts should be inexpensive.

6. **Instead / Instead of / However** wrapping gifts for Thai colleagues in white or black paper, use brightly colored paper. Bright colors signal happiness.

7. Do not surprise a Japanese colleague with a gift. **Despite / On the contrary / In spite of**, it is acceptable to surprise an American colleague with a gift.

8. In Japanese companies, you may not know your colleagues, **nonetheless / in spite of / despite**, you should bring small gifts back from your vacations for the office.

9. Don't get expensive gifts for everyone. **Despite / Instead / Instead of**, bring back some small souvenirs or snacks from your vacation to share with everyone.

3 Complete the sentences about working in another culture. Write sentences that are true for you.

1. I feel _very positive_ about working in other cultures, although

   I realize I need to learn a lot about them.

2. Younger workers should expect to _____ when

   working in my country of origin. On the other hand, older workers should expect to

   _____ .

3. In companies I am familiar with, female workers often

   _____ . Conversely, male workers often

   _____ .

4. I am very interested in working in _____ ,

   although I have never _____ .

Avoid Common Mistakes

1 Circle the mistakes.

1. Some companies translate their business cards. **In the other hand**, this can
                (a)   (b)   (c)
   be expensive.

2. In the Middle East, people may accept phone calls during **meetings. In contrast** this is
                                                  (a)   (b)   (c)
   not common in the United States.

3. Some companies have websites in two languages. **On another hand**, not all the
                                             (a)   (b)   (c)
   features are available in each language.

4. **Although** some salespeople are not **helpful, but** their products may be of high quality.
     (a)   (b)   (c)

5. Business deals can be lost **quickly. On** the **contrary** it takes weeks to build a good
                              (a)   (b)   (c)
   working relationship.

6. **Even though** you may be **full, but** you should accept the food that your host offers.
      (a)   (b) (c)

7. Many U.S. companies use social media. **At the other hand**, companies in other parts of
                                      (a)   (b)   (c)
   the world might not use these tools.

8. **Although** companies hire **experts, but** mistakes are still made in international
     (a)   (b) (c)
   business.

2 Identify the common mistakes in the sentences. Label each sentence with the type of mistake from the box. If there is no mistake, write *e*. Then correct each sentence.

---

a. Use the correct preposition with *On the other hand.*

b. Use *the other*, not *another* in *On the other hand.*

c. Remember to use a comma when transition words and phrases such as *On the contrary* and *In contrast* come at the beginning of a sentence.

d. Do not use *but* in sentences with adverb clauses of concession.

e. There is no mistake.

---

d Even though there are a variety of different business conversation styles around
(1)

the world, ~~but~~ they can be compared to three sports: basketball, bowling, and rugby.

The conversation style used in the United States is most like basketball. In this style, it's

common for speakers to jump into the conversation by talking over the others. _____ On
(2)

one hand, this is desirable because points can be made very quickly. _____ On another
(3)

hand, this can get too competitive! _____ In contrast business conversation styles in
(4)

most of Asia are more structured. These styles are similar to bowling. Speakers wait for

each other to finish before they take their turn; in addition, there are rules for who

speaks first. It's not as important for speakers to take turns in the Middle East and

Latin America. _____ On the contrary jumping in to take control of the conversation is
(5)

very common in these regions. The speaking styles in these areas are like rugby. _____
(6)

Although the rugby and basketball styles have some similarities, such as talking when

others are talking, but there are differences. _____ For example, in the rugby style, one
(7)

speaker may touch the other speaker or move closer to him or her. Touching can be

friendly and can signal agreement. _____ In the other hand, touching another person
(8)

can be seen as too personal. Speakers in the basketball style tend not to do this. _____
(9)

Perhaps the most important thing to remember about conversation styles is that they

are generalities. _____ Although many people will have the style of their culture, but
(10)

there may be differences among individuals.

Self-Assessment

Circle the word, phrase, or item that correctly completes each sentence.

1. _____ it may be frustrating to be kept waiting for a meeting, it is important to remain flexible.

   a. But   b. Although   c. Ø

2. While interruptions may be annoying, _____ they may be normal in the host's culture.

   a. though   b. whereas   c. Ø

3. It may be daunting doing business in another culture. _____ , you can relieve your fears by learning about the culture.

   a. Despite   b. Nevertheless   c. In contrast

4. Although Americans present business cards with one hand, _____ they should always present them with two hands in Asia and the Middle East.

   a. even though   b. while   c. Ø

5. In the United States, the customer is always right. _____ in Europe, the customer isn't always right.

   a. Instead of   b. Conversely,   c. Whereas

6. Specialty stores might carry higher quality products _____ the cheaper ones sold at chain stores.

   a. instead of   b. although   c. despite

7. Many business meetings are in English. _____ the other hand, participants may speak other languages instead.

   a. In   b. On   c. At

8. In the United States, casual clothing is acceptable in many workplaces, _____ this may not be true on important days.

   a. in spite of   b. although   c. Ø

9. _____ their best efforts, the American businesspeople couldn't close the deal with their Chinese partners.

   a. Despite   b. Instead of   c. In contrast,

10. _____ they may have come to an agreement, they will still need to sign a contract.

    a. Instead   b. But   c. Although

11. _____ e-mail is the most common form of communication, it is still necessary to use phones.

    a. Ø   b. Though   c. However,

12. In some cultures, smiling does not indicate acceptance of ideas. _____ it may indicate worry.

    a. Instead,　　b. Instead of　　c. While

13. _____ they have agreed to something, Japanese businesspeople may still expect to negotiate further.

    a. Despite　　b. In spite of　　c. Even though

14. In the United States, large corporations tend to be very formal, _____ some corporations in the arts or technology fields may be less formal.

    a. although　　b. Ø　　c. instead

15. China and India are known to be flexible with the beginning times of meetings. In the U.K., in _____ being on time is a sign of professionalism.

    a. contrast;　　b. contrast.　　c. contrast,

Narrative 1

The American Dream

Past Perfect and Past Perfect Progressive

1 Complete the sentences about civil rights activist Rosa Parks with the correct form of the verb in parentheses. Use the past perfect and the simple past once in each sentence. Use the adverbs and frequency expressions to help you.

Rosa Parks

1. Although African Americans in Alabama _had lived_ (live) with discrimination for centuries, segregation _became_ (become) an official part of state law in 1900.

2. By the time Rosa Parks _____ (marry), she _____ (not / receive) her high school diploma.

3. Rosa Parks _____ (succeed) in registering to vote in 1933, although she _____ (try) to register twice before unsuccessfully.

4. Rosa Parks's husband _____ (join) the NAACP, a civil rights organization, before Rosa _____ (join) in 1943.

5. Before Rosa _____ (began) working at the Maxwell Air Force Base, she _____ (not / experience) an integrated workplace.

6. In 1955, police _____ (arrest) Rosa Parks because she _____ (not / give up) her seat on the bus in the section for whites only.

7. Rosa Parks _____ (win) many awards by the time she _____ (die) in 2005.

2 Complete the sentences about women's pursuit for equal rights in the United States. Write the correct form of the verbs in parentheses. Use the past perfect progressive and the simple past once in each sentence.

Elizabeth Cady Stanton

Lucretia Mott

1. Before women <u>*got*</u> (get) the right to vote in 1920, they <u>*had been dreaming*</u> (dream) of the day for a long time.

2. Many women _____ (work) tirelessly to get the right to vote before lawmakers _____ (decide) to extend the right to women.

3. Some states _____ (consider) giving women more rights when a group of women _____ (organize) a convention in 1848 to discuss the issue in Seneca Falls, New York.

4. By the time they _____ (hold) the Seneca Falls Convention, women's rights advocates Elizabeth Cady Stanton and Lucretia Mott _____ (correspond) for years.

5. Before Elizabeth Cady Stanton _____ (decide) to attend the Seneca Falls Convention, she _____ (draft) her Declaration of Sentiments.

6. While she _____ (get) more involved in the struggle for women's rights, Elizabeth Cady Stanton _____ (hear) that Lucretia Mott would be giving a speech near her home.

7. Lucretia Mott _____ (campaign) to end slavery before she _____ (become) an advocate for women's rights.

8. Before Elizabeth Cady Stanton _____ (speak) at the Seneca Falls Convention, some people _____ (question) the need for full rights for women.

Past Modals and Modal-like Expressions

1 Complete the paragraph about the struggle for factory workers' rights in the United States. Use the words in the box. Some words may be used more than once.

could	could not	did not have to	had to

Before the rise of labor unions, factories *did not have to* ₍₁₎ provide a safe environment for workers. Factory owners _____ refuse to fix broken or unsafe equipment, ₍₂₎ and workers _____ complain about working ₍₃₎ conditions without fear of losing their jobs. If workers wanted to keep their jobs, they often _____ tolerate unsafe ₍₄₎ working conditions and poor wages.

In the 1930s, things changed when new labor laws were passed. According to these laws, workers _____ form labor unions if they wanted to, and the factory ₍₅₎ owners _____ stop them. The laws protected workers. Workers had choices, ₍₆₎ and they _____ accept unsafe working conditions if they were uncomfortable ₍₇₎ with them. However, they _____ join the labor union in order to be protected ₍₈₎ under these new laws because only workers in the labor union were protected.

2 Complete the comment board of a blog about home ownership in the United States. Circle the correct past modal.

leave a comment

1. Ten years ago, we were able to afford a house, but now we can't. We _____ bought a house then.

   a. couldn't have   b. shouldn't have   c. should have

2. Last year, more people _____ taken advantage of benefits for first-time homebuyers, but they failed to do so.

   a. shouldn't have   b. could have   c. couldn't have

3. You _____ made such a quick decision to give up your apartment. You won't have a place to live if you aren't able to buy a house you like.

   a. shouldn't have   b. couldn't have   c. could have

4. We _____ sold our house when we had a buyer a year ago! No one has made an offer since then.

   a. shouldn't have   b. couldn't have   c. should have

5. Don't feel bad about buying your house last month. You _____ known that prices would drop so much this month.

   a. couldn't have   b. shouldn't have   c. should have

6. We _____ more research about the neighborhood before we bought our home, but we ran out of time and we didn't bother.

   a. shouldn't have done   b. were going to do   c. couldn't have done

7. My wife and I _____ a new home after our wedding, but we just didn't have good enough credit. We had to rent at first.

   a. were supposed to buy   b. didn't have to buy   c. shouldn't have bought

8. My parents really regret selling their house. They feel they _____ left their old neighborhood.

   a. should have   b. shouldn't have   c. couldn't have

3 Complete the sentences about Fernanda's grandparents. Use *used to* or *would*. Sometimes both are possible.

1. When Fernanda was a young girl, her grandparents _used to/would_ talk about their lives in Mexico.

2. Her grandparents _____ own a large farm in Mexico.

3. They _____ grow vegetables and they _____ sell them in the United States.

4. Their older children _____ cross the border in order to sell the crops.

5. Their children _____ tell them to sell their farm in Mexico and move to the United States.

6. Fernanda's grandparents _____ resist this idea, but over time, they changed their minds.

7. They _____ be lonely when they first moved to the United States.

8. After they first moved, their children _____ help them with language and customs in the United States.

Common Time Clauses

1 Read about Cesar Chavez, founder of the United Farm Workers of America. Underline the adverb clauses of time/sequence in the sentences. Then label the sentences.

> 1 = the event in the time clause happened first
> 2 = the event in the time clause happened second
> ST = the events of both clauses happened at the same time
> Q = one event quickly followed another event
> RP = the events are repeated and connected
> U = the event began in the main clause in the past and continued up to a certain point or event

1. __2__ <u>Before Cesar Chavez was born</u>, his grandfather had acquired a large farm in Arizona.

2. _____ When Cesar was 10 years old, his father lost the family farm.

3. _____ After his family lost the farm, Cesar and his family had to become migrant farm workers.

4. _____ The family moved every time a crop harvest finished.

5. _____ Cesar stayed in school until he reached the eighth grade.

6. _____ Once he was 18 years old, Cesar joined the army.

7. _____ Before Cesar returned to farm work, he left the army.

8. _____ He started organizing farm workers into productive unions when he became tired of their horrible working conditions.

9. _____ He organized boycotts of grapes or other crops every time the farm workers were treated badly.

10. _____ Farm workers had very little hope for fair treatment until Cesar Chavez began leading them.

2 Complete the sentences about your life. Write sentences that are true for you.

1. When I was very young, <u>*I learned a second language*</u>.

2. After I moved _____.

3. While I was _____.

4. Until I met _____.

5. Since I started _____.

6. Before I went _____.

7. Every time _____.

Avoid Common Mistakes

1 Circle the mistakes.

1. Cory's family **had** never (live) in a big city before his father **got** a job offer in Chicago.
   (a)   (b)   (c)

2. First, they **offered** the job; then he **accepted** it, and after that, they **had moved.**
   (a)   (b)   (c)

3. He **had wrote** directly to the company president, and she **responded** immediately.
   (a)   (b)   (c)

4. He **was thinking** about changing careers for a very long time when the job offer **came** through.
   (a)   (b)   (c)

5. When the family **decided** to move, they **were planning** to buy a new house.
                (a)   (b)   (c)

6. The moving trucks **arrived** on a Monday and **had** delivered their belongings to their new
                    (a)   (b)

   home on Wednesday. The movers then **helped** them to arrange the furniture.
                                   (c)

7. Cory **called** his old friends and **had told** them about his trip to Chicago. They had **missed**
         (a)   (b)   (c)

   him a lot.

8. Before school **began**, Cory **had took** a tour of his new school.
                 (a)   (b)   (c)

2 Identify the common mistakes in the sentences. Label each sentence with the type of mistake from the box. If there is no mistake, write *d*. Then correct each sentence.

a. Remember to use the past participle after *had* when forming the past perfect.	c. Remember to use the simple past, not the past perfect, for a single completed action or state.
b. Use the past perfect progressive, not the past progressive, when the action happens in an earlier time frame.	d. There is no mistake.

                                                     written

  a Since he was a child, Drew had always ~~wrote~~ short stories. _____ Every time Drew's
 (1)   (2)

mother saw him writing, she had worried. She didn't think that his writing would lead to

a good job or financial security. _____ Drew's mother had had a boring job for years, and
                                     (3)

she didn't want to see Drew in the same situation. _____ Soon after Drew had began high
                                             (4)

school, his English teacher noticed his talent. _____ She was reading students' work for 20
                                         (5)

years when Drew's clever stories came across her desk. She was surprised at their maturity.

_____ She had never saw stories like his before. _____ At the end of his junior year, Drew's
 (6)   (7)

teacher suggested that he enter his stories in a competition. _____ He was hoping for an
                                                      (8)

opportunity like this since he was a child. All of a sudden the opportunity was there. Drew

was thrilled when his stories won first place, earning him a college scholarship.

Self-Assessment

Circle the word or phrase that correctly completes each sentence.

1. Even though we had _____ gotten ready to leave the office, our boss asked us to stay for a late meeting.

   a. still   b. just   c. earlier

2. He _____ researching the company as soon as his interview was scheduled.

   a. started   b. had been starting   c. had started

3. In order to become a professional musician, Silvia _____ practice about eight hours a day.

   a. could not   b. could   c. had to

4. Robert had always _____ of owning a farm until he found out how difficult farm life was.

   a. dream   b. dreamed   c. dreaming

5. Joe _____ preparing for his job interview for weeks.

   a. was   b. had   c. had been

6. Many civil rights activists feel they _____ achieved much without Martin Luther King, Jr.

   a. should have   b. shouldn't have   c. couldn't have

7. Victoria _____ to attend graduate school until she found her dream job.

   a. plans   b. has planned   c. had been planning

8. _____ they received their visas to the United States, they made their airline reservations.

   a. Until   b. As soon as   c. Every time

9. My parents _____ sacrificed so much for me. They had harder lives than they deserved.

   a. should have   b. shouldn't have   c. could have

10. After _____ his survey responses, Dr. Reid wrote an article for an important journal.

    a. he had received   b. he had been receiving   c. received

11. While he was _____ college in the 1950s, Joe was the only minority student.

    a. attending   b. had attended   c. had been attending

12. In the past, companies _____ provide benefits to their workers, but now they do.

    a. had to   b. did not have to   c. could

13. A century ago, immigrants _____ live in communities in the downtown area.

    a. had   b. should   c. used to

14. Jessica hadn't thought much about her finances _____ home ownership became so difficult.

    a. until   b. while   c. every time

15. Many women had _____ considered gender inequality to be an issue by the 1960s.

    a. already   b. before   c. yet

Narrative 2

Immigration

Demonstratives

1 A Complete the article about immigration. Use the words in the box.

that	These . . . are	this . . . is	Those
these	this	~~those~~	those . . . are

Throughout the seventeenth century, immigration from countries in Europe to North America grew. Life in _those_ (1) countries was often difficult, and emigration represented a chance for a new life. At _____ (2) time, most immigrants worked on farms when they reached their new country.

_____ (3) immigrants _____ (3) referred to today as settlers, because they established new settlements in our country for European immigrants.

Farming was a difficult, labor-intensive life in the early days of _____ (4) country, but many immigrants survived and in fact prospered. Many later immigrants settled in major cities. In _____ (5) cities, they often settled near relatives or others from their countries, and many cities once had a "Little Italy" or a "Chinatown," where the bulk of the residents were from one country. Many of _____ (6) old neighborhoods _____ (6) gone now, although some have survived or become centers of newer immigrant groups.

Some early immigrants were routinely discriminated against in housing and employment. _____ (7) behaviors are illegal today. However, adjusting to life in a new country is rarely easy; _____ (8) unfortunate fact _____ (8) as true for today's immigrants as it was two centuries ago for those who left their countries looking for a new life.

B Circle the correct explanation for the choice of demonstratives in A.

1. The demonstrative shows _____ .

    a. distance in time from the writer   ⓑ physical distance from the writer

    c. distance in opinion from the writer

2. The demonstrative shows _____ .

    a. a recent time   b. a very recent time   c. a distant time

3. The demonstrative shows _____ .

    a. a recent time   b. an idea the writer shares   c. a recent topic

4. The demonstrative shows _____ .

    a. closeness in space   b. closeness in time   c. distance in space
       to the writer   to the writer   from the writer

5. The demonstrative shows _____ .

    a. closeness in space   b. a recent time   c. a recent topic

6. The demonstrative shows _____ .

    a. distance in time   b. distance in space   c. a recent topic

7. The demonstrative shows _____ .

    a. distance in space   b. distance in time   c. closeness in time

8. The demonstrative shows _____ .

    a. an idea the writer shares   b. a recent topic   c. a recent time

2 Complete the sentences about a community. Circle the word or phrase that correctly completes each sentence.

1. I think you will like _____ neighborhood; this area has a lot of immigrant-owned businesses.

    ⓐ this   b. these   c. that

2. There are some beautiful old buildings on Main Street. Some of those buildings, like the school and the post office, are over 100 years old. _____ are kept in good shape.

    a. Those buildings   b. These new places   c. This building

3. Fifteen years ago, this neighborhood was in bad shape, with a lot of abandoned houses. _____ is no longer the case now, though.

    a. this   b. that   c. these

4. As you can see, today there is a new community. _____ community has a variety of new stores.

    a. this   b. these   c. that

5. Some residents don't like the new businesses and think they should be restricted. _____ stems from a fear of outsiders.

   a. That phenomenon   b. This controversial argument   c. That undisputable fact

6. Studies have shown that immigrant businesses have improved our economy. _____ was proven in our local paper last week.

   a. This questionable fact   b. This indisputable fact   c. That undisputable fact

7. _____ businesses are new, but many of the business owners have lived here for a long time.

   a. These   b. Those   c. This

8. It isn't easy to move to a new country. I remember _____ feeling from my own past.

   a. this   b. that   c. those

Common Time Signals

1 Complete the sentences about the U.S. population. Circle the word or phrase that correctly completes each sentence.

1. This graph shows a summary of the foreign-born population in the United States _____ about 150 years.

   a. from   b. through   ⓒ over the course of

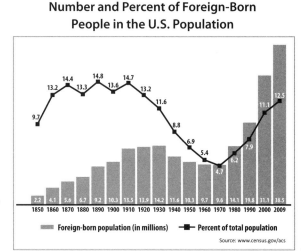

Number and Percent of Foreign-Born People in the U.S. Population

2. According to the graph, the number of foreign-born people in the United States increased _____ about 1930, and then declined.

   a. through   b. after   c. by

3. The percent of total population who were foreign-born was at its lowest _____ 1960 _____ 1980.

   a. over … to   b. for … to   c. from … through

4. The number of foreign-born residents was 9.6 million in the 1970s; that's about the same as it was _____ .

   a. 10 years earlier   b. 10 years for   c. since the 1970s

5. The foreign-born population dropped below 10 million in the 1960s _____ in decades.

   a. for the first time   b. since the last time   c. for 10 years

6. The foreign-born percentage exceeded 13 percent in the 1860s; it stayed between 13 percent and 15 percent _____ 60 years.

   a. over the   b. over the next   c. over the course

7. After that, the percentage began to decrease; _____ , it totaled only 4.7 percent.

   a. since the 1970s   b. already in the 1970s   c. by the 1970s

8. In the 1980s, the percentage and number of foreign-born people began to increase _____ .

   a. for four decades   b. once again   c. this is the first time

9. The debate over immigration has heated up again _____ , and many Americans want to change immigration policies.

   a. just   b. recently   c. for the first time

10. This isn't the first time _____ about changing immigration policies, and it surely won't be the last.

   a. people have thought   b. people think   c. people are thinking

2 Complete the sentences about immigration to the United States. Match the best word to complete each sentence.

1. During World War I, immigration from Europe slowed, but there was a big increase __*d*__ the war.

2. _____ the next six years, Congress instituted a national-origins quota system as a way to control this increase.

3. _____ 1921 to 1924, Congress passed more restrictive laws that limited the number of newcomers from each country.

4. In 1939, World War II began. Over the _____ of the early 1940s, fear led to policies that discriminated against some groups.

5. _____ 1945, attitudes had changed somewhat, and Congress passed the War Brides Act.

6. Over _____ following the war, foreign-born spouses and families of returning soldiers were welcomed to the United States under this law.

7. Over the _____ 15 years, new laws like the Hungarian Refugee Act of 1956 and the Cuban Adjustment Program of the 1960s allowed distinct new groups into the country.

8. The year 1965 was the first _____ Congress instituted a system intended to reunite families and attract skilled workers.

9. _____ that time, there has been an increase in immigration from Asia and Central and South America.

a. course

b. the years

c. next

d. after

e. From

f. Since

g. Over

h. By

i. time

3 Unscramble the sentences about Mona's life.

1. Egypt after / Mona came to the United States from / 1996 / she finished high school in

   Mona came to the United States from Egypt after
   she finished high school in 1996.

2. for about five years / lived there / when she first arrived and / she settled in downtown Chicago

   _____

   _____

3. and over the next five years, / in a department store, / she saved her money carefully / she got a job

   _____

   _____

4. by 2002, / she had saved / be able to start college / enough money to

   _____

5. for anything else / Mona worked the entire time / that left her little time / she was in college;

   _____

6. a bachelor's degree in accounting / she attended college / when she received / from 2002 through 2007,

   _____

7. to move to the suburbs / when she got her / her new salary enabled her / first job as an accountant,

   _____

8. debating the costs and benefits, / a small house on a quiet street / after / she finally bought

   _____

9. that she missed the city / it was the first time / and she found / she had lived in such a quiet neighborhood,

   _____

10. her old friends / in the city once / now Mona is back / again, living in her old neighborhood near

    _____

4 Complete the sentences about the past. Write sentences that are true for you.

1. I lived _in Illinois_ from _2008_ through _2010_ .

2. When I came to _____ , I _____ for the first time.

3. Over the past _____ , I _____ .

4. I have been _____ for _____ .

5. Now I _____ . This is the first time I _____ .

6. Once or twice _____ .

Avoid Common Mistakes

1 Circle the mistakes.

1. Jorge left his country three years ago. **These** trip was **the first time** he **ever** had left
   (a)   (b)   (c)
   his country.

2. **These** new city is very nice. He wants to stay **over the next** few years. He had **already**
   (a)   (b)   (c)
   decided to stay before he arrived.

3. He had gotten **already** a job before he came to **this** country. He had to train
   (a)   (b)
   over the first few days.
   (c)

4. **This** computer training sessions were intense. He had **never** done **this** before.
   (a)   (b)   (c)

5. **Over past year**, he has improved his computer skills. **These** are skills he had **never**
   (a)   (b)   (c)
   learned in his home country.

6. After three years, Jorge was promoted. **This** was his first promotion. He **always** had
   (a)   (b)
   hoped for **this**.
   (c)

7. **Over next four years**, he met his wife and started a family. He **had never dreamed** of
   (a)   (b)
   starting a family. **This** made him very happy.
   (c)

8. He had **always** planned on teaching his children English and Spanish.
   (a)
   Over the next few years, he taught his children **this** languages.
   (b)   (c)

2 Identify the common mistakes in the sentences. Label each sentence with the type of mistake from the box. If there is no mistake, write *d*. Then correct each sentence.

> a. Remember to use *this*/*that* with singular nouns and *these*/*those* with plural nouns.
> b. Remember to use *the* in time signals such as *over the past year* and *in the next five years*.
> c. Remember that many adverbs of time are usually placed before the main verb but after the verb *be*.
> d. There is no mistake.

a There's a new museum in our city; its first exhibit is on the history of the
(1)
          this
settlement of ~~these~~ area. _____ I visited this museum last weekend; I wanted to see their
          (2)

"living history" show. _____ In these show, actors play people from periods in our city's
          (3)

history; they were wearing clothes and doing tasks from that time. _____ I had seen never
          (4)

such amazing re-enactors. _____ One played a recent immigrant who was working for a
          (5)

married couple; this immigrant was a distant relative. _____ Those show demonstrated how
          (6)

much work it was for new immigrants to come here. _____ I'm planning to visit the museum
          (7)

again over next few months for its other exhibits. _____ The one over next two weeks is
          (8)

going to be particularly interesting. _____ I always am interested in learning new things from
          (9)

these exhibits.

Self-Assessment

Circle the word or phrase that correctly completes each sentence.

1. At one time, immigration to the United States was primarily from Europe, but _____ was a long time ago.

   a. this   b. it   c. that

2. The adults in my family sometimes talk about our early days in this country. We have a lot of fun remembering _____ times.

   a. these   b. those   c. the

3. Some people claim that U.S. borders should be closed to all immigration; however, most people do not support _____ controversial argument.

   a. it   b. this   c. that

4. New immigrants often don't speak fluent English; _____ can lead to discrimination against them.

   a. this   b. these immigrants   c. this language

5. Finding a job and settling into a new place are difficult. _____ are even more difficult in an unfamiliar language.

   a. This challenge   b. These challenges   c. These reasons

6. The subject of restricting immigration is popular on radio talk shows. _____ usually brings out strong, conflicting opinions.

   a. This aspect   b. This undisputed fact   c. This controversial topic

7. The Statue of Liberty was given to the United States by France. Dedicated in 1886, _____ has taken on the role of a familiar welcoming symbol for immigrants and visitors.

   a. these   b. it   c. since then

8. The artist who designed the statue gave it the name Statue of Liberty Enlightening the World; _____ usually abbreviated to Statue of Liberty.

   a. this is   b. these are   c. this

9. The statue stands on a small island in New York Harbor. _____ , it was renamed Liberty Island in 1956.

   a. Once   b. Once called Liberty Island   c. Once called Bedloe's Island

10. Patterns of migration have changed _____ 100 years.

    a. over the past   b. since the past   c. by the past

11. For many immigrants, settling in their new country is the first time _____ away from family.

    a. they are living   b. they live   c. they have lived

12. _____ , most immigrants become comfortable in their new country.

    a. The first time   b. Over time   c. Years earlier

13. The Tenement Museum in New York City has been conducting guided tours of the buildings _____ over 20 years.

    a. since   b. by   c. for

14. The museum's founders had been searching for a location for their museum for years. _____ 1988, they were ready to give up the search.

    a. By   b. Since   c. Once

15. Fortunately, they stumbled upon 97 Orchard Street, an old tenement that was the perfect place. _____ then, they have devoted themselves to recreating the tenements and educating the public about life for immigrants in the past two centuries.

    a. Once   b. Since   c. For

The Passive

1 Read the sentences about Nicholas's job interview. Then label each sentence.

> AS = active sentence   PS = passive sentence

1. _AS_ Nicholas had a job interview last week at a small company not too far from his home.

2. _____ The company had advertised for an office assistant; Nicholas had some experience in an office.

3. _____ The application had to be submitted online.

4. _____ About two weeks later, Nicholas was called in for an interview at the company's main location.

5. _____ He felt nervous because he didn't know what to expect.

6. _____ He was greeted by the office manager and asked to sit in the conference room.

7. _____ The interview was conducted by a panel of three employees.

8. _____ After he'd responded to all of their questions, Nicholas had a chance to ask some questions of his own.

9. _____ Then he was given a short tour of the office.

10. _____ Nicholas was told that he would be contacted within a week.

11. _____ Despite his initial nervousness, Nicholas felt that the interview had gone well.

12. _____ Yesterday, Nicholas was offered the position.

2 Complete the sentences about filling job openings. Circle the word or phrase that correctly completes each sentence.

1. This is the process used when job openings _____ at the college where I work.

   (a.) are filled   b. fill   c. is filled

2. When a position is open or available, the first thing that happens is that the position _____ online.

   a. are advertised   b. is advertised   c. was advertised

3. It _____ to the newspaper, too, if it's a high-level position.

   a. may be sent   b. may send   c. sends

4. Some positions _____ as "Internal Candidates Only"; that means there are enough good candidates already working at the college.

   a. are classified   b. classified   c. classify

5. These positions _____ to non-employees.

   a. not offered   b. is being offered   c. will not be offered

6. After a position _____ as "open" for two weeks, it is closed.

   a. was listed   b. has been listed   c. lists

7. At that point, no more applications _____ .

   a. are accepted   b. accepted   c. is accepted

8. Then all of the applications _____ by a review committee; the committee eliminates any applicants who are not qualified.

   a. evaluated   b. is evaluated   c. are evaluated

9. The highest-rated applicants _____ to interview, usually with a panel of four or five employees.

   a. are invited   b. invited   c. to be invited

10. Once all of the interviews _____ , the panel recommends its top choices to the supervisor.

    a. have held   b. was being held   c. have been held

11. The best applicant _____ .

    a. is selected   b. selected   c. has been selected

12. Finally, he or she _____ the position.

    a. offers   b. is offered   c. is being offered

3 Complete the sentences about performance-based interviews. Circle the phrase that best completes each sentence.

1. An interview in which candidates are asked about their past behavior

   (a.) is referred to as a performance-based interview.

   b. refers to a performance-based interview.

   c. is being referred to as a performance-based interview.

2. Performance-based interviewing is based on the fact that past behavior

   a. can't be shown to be the best predictor of future behavior.

   b. should have been shown to be the best predictor of future behavior.

   c. has been shown to be the best predictor of future behavior.

3. A performance-based interview is structured so that examples of past behavior

   a. is elicited.

   b. can be elicited.

   c. may have been elicited.

4. In a performance-based interview, the applicant

   a. is asked to describe what he or she has done in a specific situation.

   b. described what he or she has done in a specific situation.

   c. is describing what he or she has done in a specific situation.

5. With the types of questions that are used in a performance-based interview, interviewees

   a. are asked to discuss their experiences, not their ideas.

   b. had discussed their experiences, not their ideas.

   c. had been required to discuss their experiences, not their ideas.

6. In this type of interview, most of the talking

   a. has been done by the applicant.

   b. was done by the applicant.

   c. is done by the applicant.

7. The difference between this kind of interview and a more traditional one

   a. can illustrate the type of answers each one requires.

   b. can be illustrated by the type of answers each one requires.

   c. could have been illustrated by the type of answers each one requires.

8. For instance, instead of the question, "How would you interact with an upset co-worker?" the question, "Tell me about a time when you had to interact with an upset co-worker"

   a. should have been included.

   b. was included.

   c. would be included.

9. Traditional methods choose candidates based on what they say they *would* do; better results

   a. can be obtained by asking candidates what they have actually done.

   b. had been obtained by asking candidates what they have actually done.

   c. ask candidates what they have actually done.

10. Moreover, in a performance-based interview, the potential employee

    a. gives a more accurate picture of the duties involved in the job.

    b. is given a more accurate picture of the duties involved in the job.

    c. was being given a more accurate picture of the duties involved in the job.

4 Rewrite the job interview guidelines using the passive form.

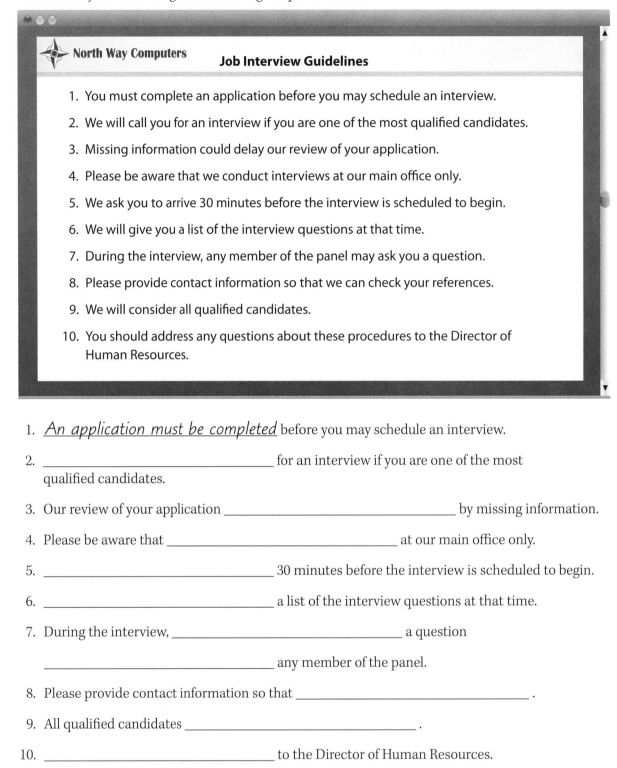

North Way Computers   **Job Interview Guidelines**

1. You must complete an application before you may schedule an interview.

2. We will call you for an interview if you are one of the most qualified candidates.

3. Missing information could delay our review of your application.

4. Please be aware that we conduct interviews at our main office only.

5. We ask you to arrive 30 minutes before the interview is scheduled to begin.

6. We will give you a list of the interview questions at that time.

7. During the interview, any member of the panel may ask you a question.

8. Please provide contact information so that we can check your references.

9. We will consider all qualified candidates.

10. You should address any questions about these procedures to the Director of Human Resources.

1. _An application must be completed_ before you may schedule an interview.

2. _____ for an interview if you are one of the most qualified candidates.

3. Our review of your application _____ by missing information.

4. Please be aware that _____ at our main office only.

5. _____ 30 minutes before the interview is scheduled to begin.

6. _____ a list of the interview questions at that time.

7. During the interview, _____ a question

_____ any member of the panel.

8. Please provide contact information so that _____ .

9. All qualified candidates _____ .

10. _____ to the Director of Human Resources.

5 Complete the article about studies on interviews. Use the correct form of the words in the box.

analyze	argue	associate	be	~~carry out~~	compare	link	observe

Studies that have been _carried out_ on interviewing have produced some interesting
(1)

results, from a legal point of view. When data have _____ , clear lessons
(2)

have sometimes emerged. One example is a comparison of common interview formats.

When unstructured interviews were _____ to structured interviews, they
(3)

_____ found to produce less consistent results. That is, unstructured interviews
(4)

are _____ with wider variations in panel members' opinions. Thus, it can
(5)

_____ that rigidly following a set of questions leaves hiring decisions less open
(6)

to a legal challenge.

Another issue is how interviewer's recommendations are _____ to their
(7)

feelings about candidates. It has _____ that some interviewers favor applicants
(8)

who seem most like themselves. This behavior also must be avoided if the interview process

is to be fair and open.

Common Words and Phrases Used in Classification Writing

1 Complete the sentences about community colleges. Match the phrases to correctly complete each sentence.

1. Community colleges often offer two types of programs: _b_ .

2. Depending on a student's goals, _____ .

3. Some colleges are able to offer part-time employment to their students, usually in _____ .

4. Services available at many colleges include both _____ .

5. A college's career center can provide assistance in a number of areas, _____ .

6. The advantages of working part-time while in college _____ .

a. clerical positions, library positions, and food service positions

b. credit and non-credit

c. including help with résumé writing and with job hunting

d. tutoring with academic subjects and career support services

e. include gaining job experience and learning new skills

f. a college can offer a number of options

2 Complete the sentences about organizational structures. Circle the phrase that best completes each sentence.

1. Most organizations have a structure that divides their employees into departments, and employees are assigned tasks _____ to their department.

   (a.) according   b. based   c. depending

2. In large organizations, each employment area or division is named _____ of the work it does, such as accounting, sales, and human resources.

   a. based   b. according   c. on the basis

3. The human resources department normally handles a _____ of functions related to employees and employment.

   a. consists   b. combination   c. basis

4. Most organizations also divide employees into groups _____ to their level of responsibility.

   a. according   b. based   c. depending

5. Depending on the level of each one's position, employees can be _____ employment categories.

   a. divided   b. divided into   c. divide

6. Each employment category can be _____ several levels of positions.

   a. consist of   b. involve   c. made up of

7. Job titles are assigned to positions _____ the duties and tasks the position requires.

   a. based on   b. on the basis   c. consisting of

8. Rates of pay can be at different levels, _____ how long the individual has worked for the company.

   a. depending on   b. on the basis   c. divided into

9. Experts recommend researching industry standards of pay and responsibility before going to an interview, _____ the type of job you are interviewing for.

   a. based on   b. is composed of   c. is divided into

10. Preparing for an interview _____ being ready to answer questions, but also being ready to ask them.

   a. consists of not   b. involves not only   c. is composed

3 Complete the sentences about education and jobs. Write sentences that are true for you.

1. The jobs I am most interested in fall into several categories, including _art, fashion, and theater_.

2. The educational institutions I have attended so far include _____ .

3. In my opinion, there are _____ kinds of employees in most workplaces:

_____ .

4. For me, a good job involves _____ .

5. As an employee, I have many skills. These are _____

_____ .

6. My job skills can be divided into several categories, including _____

_____ .

Avoid Common Mistakes

1 Circle the mistakes.

1. An interviewer's opinion **can frequently be** (**based in**) an applicant's personal
   <u>(a)</u>   (b)

   appearance, **so** first impressions are important.
     (c)

2. During interviews, candidates **will be frequently** **asked** why they are **interested in**
       (a)   (b)   (c)

   the position.

3. You **might be asked** to give an example of a time when you **were involved** **on** a
      (a)   (b)   (c)

   difficult or challenging situation.

4. To ensure fairness, the same questions **that are given** to the first candidate
           (a)

   must be always given to each subsequent candidate involved **in** the interview process.
       (b)   (c)

5. If a company believes that candidates **always should** **be evaluated** by several people, a
           (a)   (b)

   team interview **will probably be used**.
         (c)

6. In some situations, people who **will later be** **supervised by** the applicant are
       (a)   (b)

   involved for his or her interview.
      (c)

7. Job applicants may not **be told** what factors a hiring decision is **based** **in**.
        (a)   (b) (c)

8. If you **have never been** interviewed by a group of people, the experience
     (a)

   can be challenging the first time **you are involved by** it.
      (b)   (c)

2 Identify the common mistakes in the sentences. Label each sentence with the type of mistake from the box. If there is no mistake, write *d*. Then correct each sentence.

> a. Remember to place the adverb after the modal in passive sentences.
> b. Remember to use the correct preposition in the phrase *based on*.
> c. Remember to use the correct preposition in *involved in*.
> d. There is no mistake.

d One common type of question that is asked in interviews, both structured and
(1)

unstructured, is about strengths and weaknesses. _____ Applicants often may be asked to
(2)

talk about what they think their strong points and weak points are, based on the position

they are applying for. _____ It's a good idea to give some thought to this question if you are
(3)

going to be involved on a job interview. _____ When you are asked about your strengths,
(4)

try to talk about the skills you have, based in your experience. _____ You always should
(5)

be careful not to sound too proud, but if you have good skills, you should mention them.

_____ In some cultures it's considered impolite to say good things about yourself, but the
(6)

interviewer will be expecting you to do so. _____ One idea is to talk about any special
(7)

projects you have been involved. _____ You may be asked to talk about your weaknesses; in
(8)

this case, be honest but not negative. _____ The best answer may be one that is based as a
(9)

positive; for example, "I sometimes spend too much time on a project because I am trying

to do a good job."

Self-Assessment

Circle the word or phrase that correctly completes each sentence.

1. A good practice interview simulates the conditions that _____ in a real interview.

   a. will experience   b. experienced   c. will be experienced

2. At a conventional job interview, you can expect _____ about your employment
   history.

   a. to be asked   b. to ask   c. asked

3. Are interviewers _____ questions about your physical condition in an interview?

   a. allow to include   b. including   c. allowed to include

4. During the interview yesterday, Tomas _____ about his professional goals.

   a. was asked   b. has been asked   c. had been asked

5. Michelle knew that she _____ to write a piece of computer code during her interview for a programming position.

   a. might expect   b. might be expected   c. expected

6. Cristina has been _____ serve on an interview panel for a new position in her department.

   a. asked to   b. asked   c. asking

7. What do you think the manager's decision was _____?

   a. based on   b. suggested   c. based

8. In my opinion, this is a good company to work for, _____ other places I have worked.

   a. compared   b. compare   c. compared to

9. Which of these _____ of interviews have you participated in?

   a. topics   b. types   c. several

10. Depending on _____ conducting an interview, it can be one-on-one or a panel interview format.

    a. the classification of   b. the basis of   c. the number of people

11. Interviews are often _____ answering questions and demonstrating knowledge or skills.

    a. involving   b. a combination of   c. composed

12. There are a number of different ways to find a job, _____ looking online, researching the field, and talking to friends and acquaintances.

    a. including   b. consist of   c. involves

13. It has _____ that successful job applicants use a variety of strategies, and persist even when the search is discouraging.

    a. often observed   b. been often observed   c. often been observed

14. Applicants for job interviews are selected _____ to their skills and experience.

    a. according   b. depending   c. involving

15. Interviewers may use a number of techniques, _____ tests and presentations.

    a. which   b. which include   c. which are included

12 Classification and Definition 2

Your Ideal Job

The Language of Definition

1 Read the paragraphs about personality types. Then label the words in bold in each sentence.

GN = general noun	DD = defining details	T = term

T **Personality types** are a way of dividing people
(1)

into groups to better understand them. For example,

an individual may be a *people person*. This is someone

_____ **who enjoys the company of other people**
(2)

and is very social. People in this group are also called

_____ **extroverts**; they usually prefer to work and relax
(3)

with others. The opposite personality type is called an

_____ **introvert**. An introvert is a person _____ **who**
(4)   (5)

generally prefers to work alone.

Holland's Hexagon Model is one example of a

_____ **personality type system**. This is a _____ **system**
(6)   (7)

which divides people into six broad categories. Among

the best-known personality systems is the Myers-

Briggs Type Indicator, which divides people into 16

personality types.

Many people are curious about their personality type. One kind of personality

assessment tool is a quiz. A _____ **quiz** that gives the test taker his or her score
(8)

immediately is a self-scoring quiz. These are easy to take and readily available online.

2 Complete the sentences about the workplace. Circle the phrase that correctly completes each sentence.

1. The skills and knowledge that allow a person to do a task or job _____ *know-how*.

   (a.) is referred to as   b. refers as   c. is referred to

2. According to the U.S. Department of Labor, employment know-how _____ competencies and foundation skills.

   a. are combinations of   b. is a combination of   c. that is a combination of

3. _____ effective workers can do.

   a. Competencies are   b. Competencies are   c. Competencies
      things that   things who   means

4. One workplace competency is the ability to use resources effectively; for example, an effective worker is one who uses _____ well.

   a. its time   b. their time   c. his or her time

5. Another important competency is using interpersonal skills; these _____ working well with others.

   a. are a skill that involves   b. is a skill that involves   c. are skills that involve

6. An employee with good interpersonal skills can work well even with co-workers who are not from _____ .

   a. his or her culture   b. their culture   c. his culture

7. The ability to use technology and tools appropriately _____ .

   a. are called technology   b. is known as technology   c. technology
      competencies   competency   competency

8. An effective worker needs to be able to work with systems. _____ understanding, designing, and improving systems, and being able to monitor and improve performance.

   a. These are defined as   b. This skill is defined as   c. Defined as

9. _____ the ability to get and evaluate data; to organize, interpret, and communicate information.

   a. An information   b. Information   c. Information
      competency   competency is   competency
      defines as

3 Unscramble the sentences about stereotypes.

1. a fixed idea / is defined as / about a group of people / a stereotype

   A stereotype is defined as a fixed idea about a group of people.

2. a stereotypical member of the group / fits this idea / a person who / is sometimes referred to as

   _____

3. as a stereotypical extrovert / might be referred to / for example, a person who / loves being with others and hates being alone

   _____

4. is called / putting people into groups / based on these ideas / stereotyping

   _____

5. treating people less well / discrimination / because they are members of a particular group / is known as

   _____

6. of discrimination / a type / stereotyping / can be defined as

   _____

7. as treating people differently / is defined / gender discrimination / depending on whether they are male or female

   _____

8. their age is called / making judgments or decisions / about people based on / age discrimination

   _____

4 Complete the sentences about John Holland's system (See pp. 172 of your Student's Book for more information.). Use the passive.

1. We call a shape that represents an idea, like John Holland's hexagonal shape, a model.

   A shape that represents an idea , like John Holland's hexagonal shape,

   is called a model .

2. In Holland's system, he refers to the six personality types as artistic, investigative, realistic, social, enterprising, and conventional.

   In Holland's system, _____ artistic, investigative, realistic, social, enterprising, and conventional.

3. In Holland's theory, he calls people who like to solve problems investigative personality types.

   In Holland's theory, _____ investigative personality types.

4. It defines people with skills in working with records and numbers as having a conventional personality type.

People with skills in working with records and numbers

_____ having a conventional personality type.

5. People refer to people (or things) that get along well or work well together as compatible.

People (or things) that get along well or work well together

_____ .

6. We would define incompatible people as people who do not get along well.

_____ people who do not get along well.

7. In Holland's theoretical model, we refer to the two environments closest to each personality type as compatible environments.

In Holland's theoretical model, the two environments closest to each personality type

_____ compatible environments.

8. When ideas about human behavior seem likely but would be difficult to prove, people often call them theories.

When ideas about human behavior seem likely but would be difficult to prove,

_____ .

Appositives

1 Complete the sentences about personality types. Circle the phrase that best completes each sentence.

1. Personality instruments, _____ , can help you choose a satisfying job or field of study.

   a. are assessments used to show an individual's preferences or personality type

   b. assessments used to show an individual's preferences or personality type

   c. assessments show an individual's preferences or personality type

2. One well-known personality instrument is the Keirsey Temperament Sorter, _____ .

   a. theories developed by David Keirsey

   b. theory developed by David Keirsey

   c. a theory developed by David Keirsey

3. This instrument is designed to give insight into a person's _____ .

   a. temperament (the aspects of our personality that determine moods and behavior)

   b. temperament, (the aspects of our personality that determine moods and behavior)

   c. temperament the aspects of our personality that determine moods and behavior

4. Another popular instrument is the _____ .

   a. Myers-Briggs Type Indicator, (MBTI)

   b. Myers-Briggs Type Indicator (MBTI)

   c. Myers-Briggs Type Indicator, (MBTI),

5. Both the Keirsey Temperament Sorter and the Myers-Briggs Type Indicator are based on the work of Carl Jung, _____ .

   a. a Swiss psychiatrist who lived from 1875 to 1961

   b. a way of dividing people into personality groups

   c. two psychiatrists from Switzerland

6. These instruments are similar in that they measure preferences – _____ – not skills.

   a. what we are very good at

   b. what we prefer to measure

   c. what we prefer to do when we have a choice

7. Both instruments categorize people according to the way they process information and interact with their social environment (_____).

   a. which is the information around them

   b. meaning the air, water, and land

   c. the world they live or work in

8. Personality types should never be seen as good or bad; each type has the same potential – _____ – as every other type.

   a. the ability to develop and succeed

   b. a type of potential

   c. a better type of personality

9. For example, kinesthetic learners _____ can learn things just as well as any other learner.

   a. , people who learn best through movement

   b. who are people who learn best through movement –

   c. , people who learn best through movement,

2 Match the phrases to correctly complete each sentence.

1. The idea of different types of personalities, a popular theory in the study of psychology, _d_ .

2. Among my co-workers, _____ , there are several different personality types.

3. Kelly, our office manager, _____ .

4. Rodrigo, _____ , likes working with numbers and is an expert with budgets.

5. Jin Sun is a perfect illustration of a social personality type, _____ , so she is a great receptionist.

6. Isabel hates writing monthly reports; people with her personality type – _____ – don't like structured activities or tasks.

7. I guess I'm the investigative type. I enjoy solving problems (_____).

8. Our work requires a lot of collaboration (_____) and dedication.

9. I think that our compatibility (our ability to get along and work well together) _____ .

a. a group of people who have worked together for years

b. is due to our understanding each others' personality types

c. something I find myself having to do frequently

d. comes alive in many workplace situations

e. artistic and creative people

f. is really well organized and can find anything you need

g. working together on projects

h. a person who is good at working with people

i. our accountant and data manager

3 Rewrite the sentences about Tina. Use an appositive for the words in bold. Also use the punctuation in parentheses.

1. Tina is **my cousin** and she is very good at helping people. (commas)

   Tina, my cousin, is very good at helping people.

2. She's a good example of a social personality type; that is **a personality type that enjoys working with others**. (parentheses)

   _____

   _____

3. Tina does human resources work; this is **work helping other employees and job applicants**. (parentheses)

   _____

4. Tina works in the Employee Relations Support Office; they call it **ERSO**. (parentheses)

   _____

5. Her job is full-time; it's **40 hours a week**. (parentheses)

   _____

6. She's a Human Resources Specialist; that is **a mid-level position**. (comma)

   _____

7. At her company, a personality assessment is given to all new employees; it's called **the Workplace Compatibility Inventory**. (commas)

   _____

8. Tina says that the WCI is **a test researched and designed by her company** and that it helps people work together. (dashes)

   _____

4 Complete the sentences using appositives. Write sentences that are true for you.

1. <u>Rice</u> , one of the most popular foods in my country, is <u>both delicious and nutritious</u> .

2. The president of the United States, _____ , is

   _____ .

3. I like going to _____ , a great place for

   _____ , because _____ .

4. My professor, a person who _____ ,

   _____ .

5. My closest friend, _____ , is

   _____ .

6. My home country, _____ , produces

   _____ , and _____ .

Avoid Common Mistakes

1 Circle the mistakes.

1. What **personal characteristics** are **defined** as (**the one**) that good leaders should have?

(a)   (b)   (c)

2. Two skills **that leaders should have** are the ability to lead people and the ability to lead

(a)

change. **They** need to have **both of** them.

(b)   (c)

3. Leading people **are define** as being able to guide **others** to work effectively to meet the

(a)   (b)

goals **that** the organization has established.

(c)

4. Leading people **includes** managing any disagreements or difficult interpersonal

(a)

situations **who** may come up; this **is called** conflict management.

(b)   (c)

5. Thought leaders **are a person who** influence the way others view an issue.

(a) (b) (c)

6. People who **are** good at leading change **use** creativity and innovation to motivate

(a)   (b)

employees; they encourage others to use **them**, too.

(c)

7. Another important skill, leveraging diversity, **defines** as leading a workplace where

(a)

individual differences **are valued**.

(b)   (c)

8. A leader **which** does not have **these** skills will not be as successful as one who **does**.

(a)   (b)   (c)

2 Identify the common mistakes in the sentences. Label each sentence with the type of mistake from the box. If there is no mistake, write *e*. Then correct each sentence.

---

a. Remember to use singular and plural nouns correctly in definitions.

b. Remember to use the correct verb form in the passive when giving definitions.

c. Remember to use the correct pronoun in relative clauses. Specifically, remember to use *who* only with animate nouns.

d. Be sure that pronoun use is clear.

e. There is no mistake.

---

        a skill

<u>*a*</u> Effective leadership is ~~skills~~ that is important not only in the workplace, but in
(1)

the community as well. _____ Leading people and leading change are two skills who
      (2)

leaders need to have. _____ They are not the only ones. _____ Effective leaders need to
   (3)   (4)

be accountable, or willing to hold themselves responsible for both good work and for

mistakes. _____ They need to be what are referred to as "politically savvy"; that is, able
   (5)

to act appropriately according to the internal and external politics at work in the

organization. _____ A leader which is not able to do this is likely to run into difficulties.
      (6)

_____ Leaders need business acumen, which is defining as the ability to manage human,
(7)

money, and information resources well. _____ Without them, it is difficult to manage an
        (8)

organization. _____ Finally, a good leader needs to be results driven; this means that he
   (9)

or she is people who meet goals and expectations. _____ A person who has all of these
       (10)

skills is likely to be effective at what he or she does, and a good leader.

Self-Assessment

Circle the word or phrase that correctly completes each sentence.

1. Psychologists are _____ study human behavior.

   a. specialists   b. who   c. specialists who

2. A personality type assessment is an instrument that helps individuals find _____ personality type.

   a. his   b. her   c. their

3. Linguistic, logical/mathematical, and musical/rhythmic are three _____ intelligences.

   a. types of   b. types   c. type of

4. Spatial intelligence is ____ the ability to understand space and the relationships between things in space.

   a. called   b. defined as   c. referred to

5. Howard Gardner, a psychologist and ____ the author of the theory of multiple intelligences.

   a. researcher, is   b. researcher is   c. researcher, he is

6. Gardner's approach ____ identifies nine different intelligences.

   a. , a psychological   b. , a psychological   c. a psychological
      breakthrough   breakthrough,   breakthrough

7. In Gardner's system, interpersonal intelligence ____ the ability to understand other people.

   a. defined   b. is defined   c. is defined as

8. The ability to use language to express yourself and to understand others is ____ linguistic intelligence.

   a. called   b. referred to   c. defined as

9. A self-aware person is one who has a realistic picture and opinion of ____ abilities and personality.

   a. the   b. his or her   c. their

10. Employees in an organization's workforce are sometimes ____ to as its *human capital*.

    a. called   b. referred   c. defined

11. The feeling that the work one does is worthwhile and rewarding ____ job satisfaction.

    a. is known as   b. known as   c. knows as

12. Finding a career that fits with your ____ is likely to increase your job satisfaction.

    a. type (personality   b. type personality   c. type, (personality
       or intelligence)   or intelligence   or intelligence)

13. Talking with a career counselor ____ individual who is trained to help you identify possible careers, is always a good idea.

    a. and   b. , an   c. an

14. People who are self-possessed generally don't display ____ emotions in public.

    a. his   b. his or her   c. their

15. An auditory learner is someone who uses ____ sense of hearing to absorb and process information.

    a. its   b. his or her   c. their

Problem–Solution 1
Food and Technology

Present Perfect and Present Perfect Progressive

1 Unscramble the sentences about genetically modified (GM) foods.

1. product / eaten / modified / you / genetically / a / have / ever

   Have you ever eaten a genetically modified product?

2. already / GM / most / foods / eaten / have / people

   Have most people already eaten GM foods?

3. a / seen / label / you / supermarket / ever / have / a / GM / in

   Have you ever seen a GM label in a supermarket?

4. labels / have / in / these / never / most / supermarkets / people / seen

   Have most people seen these labels in supermarkets?

5. never / GM / been / many / have / ingredients / able / to / consumers / identify

   Many consumers have never been to able to identify GM ingrid.?

6. have / supermarkets / many / foods / labeled / not / GM / yet

   Have many supermarkets not labeled GM foods yet?

7. has / the / labels / already / GM / government / proposed / food
   have

   Has governmand already proposed the GM food labels?

8. this / law / yet / become / not / has / however,

   However, this law has not become yet.

2 Complete the sentences about salmon production. Use the simple present, simple past, present perfect progressive, or present perfect form of the verbs in parentheses. Sometimes more than one answer is possible.

The Food and Drug Administration (FDA) _has received/received_ (receive) many
                                         (1)
applications for permission to genetically alter Atlantic salmon in recent weeks.

Decisions will be made in the coming months. In response to this, the FDA

___arranged___ (arrange) a public meeting to discuss the issues. In preparation for the
    (2)
meeting, the FDA _has released_ (release) information on its website about the history
                    (3)
of salmon production. Here is an excerpt:

Atlantic salmon ___has___ always
                     (4)
___been___ (be) overfished, and this trend
   (4)
___continues___ (continue) today. Because of
    (5)
its health benefits, fish consumption

have ___increased___ (increase) dramatically in the
         (6)
last 10 years. In recent years, the Atlantic salmon

population ___have decreased___ (decrease) partly
               (7)
because of this. In fact, the Atlantic salmon ___becomes___ (become) endangered in
                                                  (8)
many parts of New England today.

Fish farming _____ (provide) one answer to the problem of overfishing.
                  (9)   ed
The farming of salmon _____ (start) in Norway in the 1960s. Since then, fish
                          (10)   ed
farms ___have___ (become) one of the main sources of fish around the world. They
         (11)
___have been___ (be) very successful, despite the fact that there ___is___ (be)
   (12)   (13)
a great deal of controversy over this practice in recent years.

3 Read the web article about genetically modified animals. Circle the verb form that correctly completes each sentence.

In recent years, there **(has been)** / **is** a great deal of
(1)
interest in genetically modified animals. More and more

people **were concerned / have been concerned**
(2)
about the potential dangers of GM animals. On

Monday, the Food and Drug Administration (FDA)

has released / released a report on genetically
(3)
modified animals. The report reveals some surprising information about GM animals,

and many consumers and animal rights activists were shocked by the report.

According to the FDA, the genetic modification of animals **has not been / is not**
(4)
a new practice. People **have been using / used** GM technologies to enhance food
(5)
products since agriculture was invented thousands of years ago. Currently, scientists

have used / are using this technology to enhance the production of animals for food.
(6)

The report **is / has been** the subject of criticism since it was released on Monday.
(7)
Critics say that only the beneficial aspects of GM animals have been included. An

FDA spokesperson **denied / has been denying** this claim yesterday, saying that the
(8)
FDA received input from groups such as animal rights activists and consumers.

4 A Read the sentences about Dr. Boris Ivanov, a researcher. Write the present perfect or present perfect progressive form of the verb in parentheses. Sometimes more than one answer is possible.

Meat from genetically modified animals _has been_ (be) available for the past few years. Recently, however, scientists _have been working_ (work) on a way to create meat in a (2) laboratory. Scientists _have grow_ (grow) cells in laboratories since 1907. For the (3) last 20 years, they _have been using_ (use) this technology for medical applications. (4) One researcher, Dr. Boris Ivanov at the Bay City Institute, _have employed_ (employ) (5) this technology to create meat in a laboratory for human consumption. He _has been taken_ (take) cells from a chicken and adding to them a chemical that (6) promotes growth. His work _has resulted_ (result) in an edible meat product. (7) Laboratory meat _have received_ (receive) a great deal of attention in the news (8) media. Animal rights activists _have been_ (be) interested in the future of (9) laboratory-generated meat. Some organizations _have offered_ (offer) grants to (10) scientists who work in this area.

B Read the sentences in A again. Then answer the question.

Which sentences in A have more than one correct answer? _____

5 Rewrite the sentences. Use the present perfect passive to represent the words in bold.

1. **Companies have listed** ingredients on food packages since 1913.

   Ingredients _have been listed_ on food packages since 1913.

2. **The government has not required** GM food labeling yet.

   GM food labeling _have not been required_ yet.

3. **Companies have used** GM ingredients in many popular snack foods.

   GM ingredients _____ in many popular snack foods.

4. **Researchers have conducted** a number of studies on consumer awareness of GM ingredients.

   A number of studies _have been conducted_ on consumer awareness of GM ingredients.

5. **Researchers have collected** statistics on consumers' attitudes toward the use of GM ingredients.

   Statistics _have been collected_ on consumers' attitudes toward the use of GM ingredients.

6. **Researchers have asked** a number of people if they thought foods with GM ingredients were safe.

   A number of people _have been asked_ if they thought foods with GM ingredients were safe.

7. **Researchers have also polled** people on the benefits of labeling foods with GM ingredients.

   People _have been polled_ on the benefits of labeling foods with GM ingredients.

8. **Researchers have invited** supermarket chains and food service professionals to participate in these polls as well.

   Supermarket chains and food service professionals _have been invited_ to participate in these polls as well.

Common Noun Phrase Structures

1 Circle the noun phrase that correctly completes each sentence.

1. _____ *locavorism* is restricting food choices to locally produced items.

   a. The definition of   b. The number of   c. The effects of

2. Sustainability is _____ locavorism because it has positive effects on the environment.

   a. the rest of   b. the number of   c. the heart of

3. _____ consuming only locally produced food is to reduce the distances that food travels from farms to consumers' tables, called "food miles."

   a. The definition of   b. The purpose of   c. The amount of

4. _____ reducing food miles is to reduce our ecological footprint.

   a. The purpose of   b. The majority of   c. The number of

5. _____ reducing food miles include limiting the use of fossil fuels and bringing fresher products to consumers.

    a. The effect of   b. The number of   c. The effects of

6. _____ eating locally is gradually becoming more popular.

    a. The notion of   b. The definition of   c. The rest of

7. _____ supermarket chains have begun labeling items as "locally grown."

    a. The number of   b. The effects of   c. A number of

8. _____ labeling produce as "locally grown" is often an increase in sales.

    a. The result of   b. The majority of   c. The basis of

2 Read the paragraph about food labeling. Choose a noun phrase from the box to complete each sentence. Sometimes more than one answer is possible, and you may use some noun phrases more than once.

a number of	the importance of	the number of	the results of	the essence of
the goal of	the majority of	the purpose of	the definition of	

A poll on food labeling was recently conducted. _The purpose of/The goal of_ the (1) poll was to determine the public's awareness of the term *natural* when applied to food products. Specifically, _the purpose of_ the survey was to discover the extent to which (2) consumers understand the meaning of this term. _The results of_ the survey showed (3) that _the majority of_ the people questioned did not understand the precise meaning of (4) *natural*. _The results of_ the poll therefore indicate that consumer education is lacking (5) in this area. _The importance of_ understanding the meaning of this term is clear when (6) one is making choices at the supermarket. For example, consumers need to be aware of _A number of_ varying conditions that the term *natural* may describe. This is an issue (7) because _the number of_ products labeled "natural" may in fact contain ingredients (8) derived from natural sources, but these ingredients may have undergone processing. _____ respondents in this study who equated *natural* with concepts such as (9) "organic" or "healthy" was surprisingly high. _The definition of_ the term *natural* can be (10) understood in many ways, as can the term *organic*. _The essence of_ these ideas implies (11) healthy, unprocessed foods. However, consumers must be informed about where their produce comes from before trusting anything with an *organic* label.

3 Complete the sentences about organic produce. Write noun phrases with *that* using the words in parentheses in the correct blank.

1. _____ I am concerned about *the fact that*
      (a)   (b)
   pesticides have been proven to be harmful. (fact)

2. _____ U.S. government agencies promote
      (a)
   __*notion that*__ there is no nutritional difference
      (b)
   between organic produce and conventionally grown

   produce. (notion)

3. _____✓_____ I disagree with _____
      (a)   (b)
   organic produce is healthier than conventionally grown

   produce. (assumption)

4. Many people are not aware of __*the fact that*__
                                          (a)
   some produce labeled "organic" is actually grown on

   _____ farms that use pesticides. (fact)
         (b)

5. Many consumers base their choices on __*the idea that*__ organic farming is less harmful
                                                  (a)
   to the environment than _____ conventional farming practices. (idea)
                                    (b)

6. In most countries, __*belief that*__ organic produce is more expensive than
                              (a)
   conventionally grown produce makes it _____ unattractive for people on a
                                                   (b)
   budget. (belief)

7. A major obstacle has been _____ organic produce is simply unavailable in
                                      (a)
   _____ some communities. (fact)
         (b)

8. Now more than ever, _____ people of all income levels must have access to
                               (a)
   fresh produce has inspired _____ community organizers to bring farmers'
                                       (b)
   markets to inner city neighborhoods. (view)

4 Write sentences about three of the topics in the list using the noun phrases in the box.

the concept of	the fact that	the importance of	the purpose of
the effects of	the idea of/that	the potential consequences of	the possibility that

Topics

genetically modified animals   labeling GM food   locally produced food

genetically modified produce   laboratory-created meat   organic produce

1. _The concept of meat created in a lab is very unappealing. The possibility that consumers would buy it is ridiculous._

2. _the potential consequences of genetically modified produce can have bad impact for human's health._

3. _the effects of buying locally produced food can improve the economy of local agriculture._

4. _the importance of developing organic produce can make people quality of life better._

Avoid Common Mistakes

1 Circle the mistakes.

1. **A** number of (expert agrees) that we should **label** GM ingredients.
   (a)　　　　　(b)　　　　　　　　　　(c)

2. Recent **researches** **shows** that organic food **has** health benefits.
   　　　(a)　　　(b)　　　　　　　　　(c)

3. **This** fact that we do not know the **effects** of GM food indicates that more **research**
   (a)　　　　　　　　　　(b)　　　　　　　　　　　　　　(c)
   needs to be done.

4. **Most** consumers were not aware of **this** fact that supermarkets sell **many** foods with
   (a)　　　　　　　　　　(b)　　　　　　　　(c)
   GM ingredients.

5. A number of **scientist agrees** that industrial food production **methods** **are** harmful to
   　　　　　(a)　　　　　　　　　　　　　　　(b)　　(c)
   the environment.

6. There is a great **deal** of **informations** on the environmental effects of meat **production**.
   　　　　　(a)　　　(b)　　　　　　　　　　　　　　(c)

7. A number of **expert believes** that we should **find** **alternatives** to pesticides.
   　　　　　(a)　　　　　　　　(b)　(c)

8. A major obstacle is **this** fact that organic **produce** is more expensive than produce
   　　　　　　　(a)　　　　　　(b)
   grown with **pesticides**.
   　　　(c)

2 Identify the common mistakes in the sentences. Label each sentence with the type of mistake from the box. If there is no mistake, write *d*. Then correct each sentence.

> a. Remember that noncount nouns such as *advice, equipment, research, information, knowledge*, and *evidence* do not have plural forms.
> b. Remember to use *the fact that*, and not *this fact that*.
> c. Remember that *a number of* takes a plural count noun and plural verb.
> d. There is no mistake.

_c_ A number of ~~expert points~~ *experts point* to the benefits of eating and growing organic produce.
(1)

_____ Organic produce is produce grown without the use of pesticides. _____ There is a great
(2)   (3)

deal of informations on the negative effects of pesticides. _____ A number of scientists agree
(4)

with the fact that pesticides cause a variety of health problems in humans. _____ For example,
(5)

researches show that pesticides can cause damage to the nervous and reproductive systems

of humans. _____ A number of study shows that when children are given a diet of organic
(6)

produce, pesticide levels in their bodies drop dramatically. _____ In addition, most experts
(7)

agree with this fact that the use of pesticides is unsustainable. _____ This is because pesticides
(8)

affect the soil, as well as insects and other living creatures. _____ This fact that pesticides build
(9)

up in the soil and remain there for many years means that the soil is less able to support plant

life as time goes on. _____ There is a great deal of evidences that organic farming practices
(10)

reverse the process of soil damage, essentially keeping it clean and healthy for generations

to come.

Self-Assessment

Circle the word or phrase that correctly completes each sentence.

1. Many people have not _____ a GM label in the supermarket.

   a. saw   b. seen   c. see

2. GM foods have _____ in some countries in Europe.

   a. not been accepted   b. not accepted   c. not been accepting

3. In 2011, the Great Foods Company _____ not to sell any GM products.

   a. decided   b. has decided   c. has been deciding

4. Recently, there _____ a great deal of concern about food safety.

   a. is   b. has been   c. had

5. The FDA _____ a number of applications to genetically modify animals in recent months.

   a. receives   b. has been receiving   c. has been received

6. People have been creating meat in laboratories _____ .

   a. for several years now   b. in 2005   c. in months

7. GM ingredients _____ in a number of snack foods.

   a. have been using   b. have used   c. have been used

8. _____ consumer education is better health.

   a. The rest of   b. The goal of   c. The number of

9. _____ of *genetic engineering* is making changes to the genes of a plant or an animal.

   a. The importance   b. The fact   c. The definition

10. Consumer awareness is _____ the FDA's report on GM foods.

    a. the purpose of   b. the amount of   c. the definition of

11. The researcher, Dr. Smith, cites _____ the genetic modification of animals is not new.

    a. the amount of   b. the number of   c. the fact that

12. Some people disagree with _____ GM foods are safe.

    a. the idea the   b. the idea that   c. the idea of

13. A number of _____ that eating organic produce has health benefits.

    a. study shows   b. study show   c. studies show

14. There is a great deal of _____ on the effects of pesticides on humans.

    a. informations   b. information   c. the information

15. Few people are aware of _____ the use of GM ingredients has increased dramatically in recent years.

    a. this fact that   b. a fact that   c. the fact that

Problem–Solution 2

Children and Health

Reporting Verbs

1 A Complete the sentences about children and exercise. Use the present form of the words in the box. Sometimes more than one answer is possible.

ніжпеньхвати   *пропонувати*

| believe | describe | emphasize | show | recommend | suggest |

1. The pamphlet *describes* six strategies for improving the health and well-being of Bay City's children.

2. The city council _*descrives*_ several low-cost ways to encourage children to get more exercise.

3. Community organizers _*believe*_ that building a skateboarding park in the city will encourage children to be more active.

4. The traffic committee _*recommends*_ adding more bicycle lanes so children will be able to ride their bikes to school.

5. The committee further _*recommends*_ offering free bike safety courses.

6. The report _*emphasizes*_ the low cost of many of these proposals.

7. Experts _*belive*_ that these measures will affect the psychological health of the *zavogu* city's children, as well as their physical health.

8. Chart 1 _*shows*_ the projected cost of the projects.

9. Illustration 5 _*descrives*_ that the cost will come from taxes.

10. Mayor Green said, "I _*believe*_ these proposals will benefit the entire community."

11. He _*believes*_ that the city should start these projects as soon as possible.

12. Mayor Green _*believes*_ that the city will become a more desirable and healthier place in which to live.

B Read the sentences in A again. Then answer the question.

In which sentence in A can you add *that*? _*10*_

Community leaders suggest that the way how
to increase children activity is to build
skateboarding park in the city,

2 Complete the sentences about childhood obesity. Circle the reporting verbs that best express the meanings given.

1. neutral in tone; reporting a fact

    The CDC (2009) **reports** / **claims** that 60 percent of school-aged children consume at least one can of soda every day.

2. likely, but still uncertain

    Wu (2010) **predicts** / **suggests** that children who consume sugary drinks have a greater chance of becoming obese.

3. opinion

    However, Johnson (2010) **believes** / **shows** that there is no evidence that consuming sugar leads to obesity.

4. likely, but still uncertain

    Moreno's data (2011) **investigates** / **suggests** that reducing sugar intake reduces blood sugar levels.

5. you are unsure that this is true

    The CDC **illustrated** / **alleged** that 70 percent of obese youth had at least one risk factor for cardiovascular disease.

6. opinion

    A CDC study **reports** / **suggests** that obese children are at greater risk for psychological problems.

7. results

    Brown's study (2011) **suggests** / **demonstrates** that obese adolescents get lower scores on self-esteem assessment tests.

8. you are unsure that this is true

    A 2009 report **claims** / **shows** that the relationship between obesity and self-esteem is cultural.

9. results

    Smith (2010) **concluded** / **recommended** that there is no connection between obesity and self-esteem in certain cultures.

10. likely, but still uncertain

    Washington (2011) **proposes** / **states** that weight affects the self-esteem of girls more than boys.

3 A researcher, Ingrid Rosen, published a study on obesity in 2011. Write her opinions. Use the reporting verbs in parentheses.

1. Obesity is a cultural issue. (believe)

   Rosen believes that obesity is a cultural issue.

2. There is not necessarily a relationship between obesity and self-esteem. (argue)

   Rosen argues

3. Not all adolescents who are overweight have psychological problems. (show)

   R shows

4. Certain cultures do not consider obesity unattractive. (emphasize)

   R emphasize

5. Certain cultures do not consider obesity unhealthy. (recognize)

   R recognize

Adverb Clauses and Phrases with *As*

1 Complete the sentences about accident rates for young workers. Circle the verb that best completes the *as* phrase.

1. As **seen** / **shows** in Table 7, three factors affect the young worker accident rate.

2. As **can see** / **can be seen** in Table 8, the number of hours worked affects the youth accident rate.

3. As Chart 4 **demonstrates** / **can be demonstrated**, time of day has an effect on the youth accident rate.

4. As **shown** / **shows** in Chart 2, job training for young workers reduces the injury rate by 33 percent.

5. As **demonstrated** / **can demonstrate** by Figure 3, a higher percentage of accidents among young people occur after six working hours.

6. As Chart 4 **shown** / **shows**, young people who leave work by 6:00 p.m. have lower accident rates.

7. As Chart 2 **points out** / **shown**, accident rates increase after 6:00 p.m.

8. As **illustrates** / **illustrated** in Figure 3, young workers are 56 percent more likely to have an accident between the hours of 9 p.m. and midnight.

9. As Chart 2 **can be seen** / **points out**, an increase in the number of job training hours that young workers receive greatly reduces the chances of on-the-job accidents.

2 Look at the chart. Complete the sentences with an *as* phrase. Use the active (A) or passive (P) form of the verbs in parentheses.

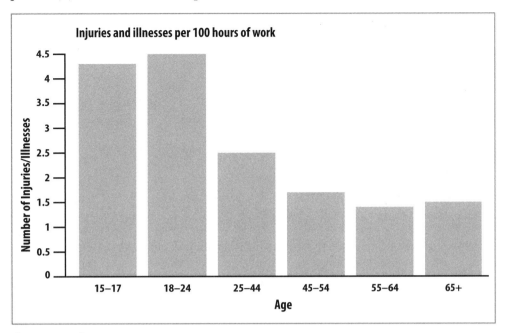

Source: www.cdc.gov

1. <u>*As the chart demonstrates*</u> , workers aged 18–24 have the highest rate of work-related injuries and illnesses. (demonstrate, A)

2. _____*As shown in chart*_____ , the rates of work-related injuries and illnesses go down after age 24. (show, P)

3. _____*As seen in chart*_____ , young workers have more work-related injuries and illnesses than older workers. (see, P)

4. _____*As the chart shows*_____ , workers aged 55–64 have the lowest rate of work-related injuries and illnesses. (show, A)

5. _____ , workers 65 and older have only 1.5 injuries and illnesses per 100 hours of work. (demonstrate, P)

6. _____ , workers aged 18–24 have 4.5 injuries and illnesses per 100 hours of work. (illustrate, A)

7. _____ , adolescent workers are more likely to suffer from work-related injuries than workers in their 30s and 40s. (illustrate, P)

8. _____ , workers aged 15–17 have a rate of 4.3 injuries and illnesses per 100 hours of work. (point out, A)

Common Vocabulary for Describing Information in Graphics

1 Look at the bar graph. Circle the word or phrase that correctly completes each sentence.

1. The bar graph **shows that / shows** the percentage of students participating in physical activity by gender and by age.

2. The graph shows that the amount of exercise boys and girls get **declines / increases** with age.

3. From the graph, it **shows / can be** concluded that girls between the ages of 14–18 get less exercise than girls between the ages of 9–13.

4. From the graph, it can be concluded that there is a **rise / decline** in participation in physical education over time.

5. From the graph, it can be seen that there is a **slight / sharp** decline in participation in family activities among adolescent girls.

6. From the graph, it can be inferred that there is a **fluctuation / drop** in the desire to exercise as children age.

7. There is a **dramatic / slow** decrease in the amount of participation in physical education between girls 9–13 and girls 14–18.

8. Participation in team sports **dropped / rose** by about 25 percent between boys 9–13 and boys 14–18.

9. There is a **steady / rapid** decrease in the amount of exercise that children get as they age.

10. There is a steep **rise / fall** in gym use for exercise as girls age.

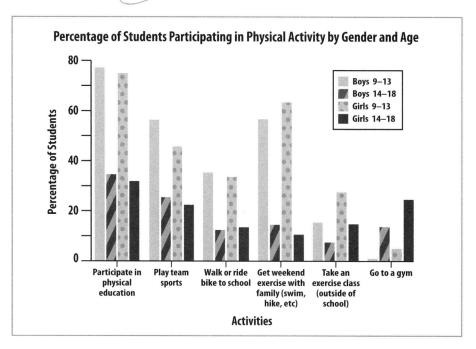

2 A Read the statements about the bar graph. Write *T* (true) or *F* (false).

1. _F_ The percentage of girls who go to a gym for exercise declines as they age.

2. _T_ Participation in family activities decreases as girls age.

3. _F_ There is a slight decrease between the percent of boys 9–13 and the percent of boys 14–18 who walk to school.

4. _F_ There is a sudden increase in participation in family exercise as boys age.

5. _T_ Participation in team sports decreases by about 23 percent as girls age.

B Write sentences about the statements in A. Use these reporting phrases: *The graph* + verb (active), *From the graph*, *it* + verb (passive).

1. _The graph shows that the percentage of girls who go to a gym for exercise increases as they age._

2. _____

3. _____

4. _____

5. _____

6. _____

Avoid Common Mistakes

1 Circle the mistakes.

1. As (the) Chart 1 **shows**, activity rates **declined** over time.
   (a)   (b)   (c)

2. From **this** study, it **can seen** **that** high school children are less active than elementary
   (a)   (b)   (c)
   school children.

3. **Table** C **shows** **that** improved health in cities with bike lanes.
   (a)   (b)   (c)

4. From **the** table, it **can inferred** **that** active families have lower body weights.
   (a)   (b)   (c)

5. As **the** Figure 1 **shows**, teenagers who do not work **miss** fewer days of school.
   (a)   (b)   (c)

6. From **the** chart, it **can seen** **that** there is a connection between genetics and
   (a)   (b)   (c)
   body weight.

7. **Table** A **shows** **that** the results of adding two hours of PE per week at three
   (a)   (b)   (c)
   public schools.

8. As **the** Chart 2 **illustrates**, people who followed the same diet had very different **results**.
   (a)   (b)   (c)

2 Identify the common mistakes in the sentences. Label each sentence with the type of mistake from the box. If there is no mistake, write *d*. Then correct each sentence.

> a. Remember to use the base form of *be* after modals in the passive.
>
> b. Remember that reporting verbs such as *show*, *demonstrate*, and *illustrate* can be followed by a *that* clause or by a noun phrase, but not by both.
>
> c. In general, when referring to a chart, graph, study, or other source with *As . . .*, do not use an article.
>
> d. There is no mistake.

_b_ A recent study shows ~~that~~ the dramatic effect that simple lifestyle changes can
(1)

have on childhood obesity and obesity-related illnesses such as high blood pressure and

Type 2 diabetes. _c_ As the Lee's 2010 study shows, children who exercised just one
(2)

additional hour per week lowered their blood pressure. _D_ As the Figure 1 shows, study
(3)

participants lowered their blood pressure by an average of 30 percent. _b_ Another
(4)

study demonstrates that a significant drop in body weight by adding only 2 hours of

activity per week. _D_ As the Figure 2 shows, 100 children lost an average of 15 pounds
(5)

in three months. _c_ From this study, it can inferred that children can achieve a steady
(6)

weight loss by increasing their activity levels only slightly. _b_ Finally, Green's 2011 study
(7)

shows that the case of a group of 150 children with Type 2 diabetes. _D_ As the Figure
(8)

3 shows, by increasing their activity levels to 30 minutes per day, over half of the children

in the group were able to stop taking diabetes medication. _c_ Clearly, the study shows
(9)

some very encouraging results. _a_ From these and other studies, it can seen that small
(10)

changes can have big results.

Self-Assessment

Circle the word or phrase that correctly completes each sentence.

1. The study _____ that 52 percent of adolescents at Bay School are overweight.

   a. reported   b. recommended   c. predicted

2. The report _____ 10 factors that cause obesity in children.

   a. shows that   b. states that   c. describes

3. Smith (2011) _____ that obesity among children has increased in the past 15 years.

   a. describes   b. reports   c. investigates

4. In his very thorough and convincing study, Ruiz (2009) _____ that consuming low fat foods contributes to obesity.

   a. alleges   b. shows   c. recommends

5. Yee (2010) _____ obesity is genetic.

   a. can be shown   b. believes that   c. displays that

6. Fine (2012) _____ that obesity is caused by a virus, but no one has proven this yet.

   a. claims   b. estimates   c. demonstrates

7. The chart _____ the six major causes of obesity.

   a. shows that   b. shows   c. is shown

8. As _____ by the graph, the rates of obesity in this group are higher among boys than girls.

   a. demonstrated   b. demonstrates   c. Figure 1 demonstrates

9. As can _____ , students' physical fitness declined when PE class was reduced to three days a week.

   a. be seen in Chart A   b. shown in Chart A   c. Chart A shows

10. From the chart, it can _____ that lack of physical education has a direct connection to obesity.

   a. infer   b. be inferred   c. infers that

11. The rate of participation went from 2 percent to 42 percent over five weeks. There was a(n) _____ in the number of students who participated.

   a. fluctuation   b. drop   c. increase

12. There was a _____ in obesity among the study participants. Ninety-five percent of the students in the study lost 35 pounds or more.

   a. sharp drop   b. sharp rise   c. slight increase

13. As _____ shows, children who participate in after-school sports have lower body weights than children who do not.

   a. Table C   b. a Table C   c. the Table C

14. From this study, it _____ that not consuming sugary soft drinks results in lower body weights.

   a. can see   b. can be seen   c. seen

15. This research clearly _____ link between body weight and blood pressure.

   a. demonstrates that a   b. demonstrates   c. demonstrates a

Problem–Solution 3

Health and Technology

Adverb Clauses of Purpose and Infinitives of Purpose

1 Complete the sentences about the Healthy Lifestyle website. Write *so* or *so that* in the correct blanks. Sometimes both answers are possible. Capitalize the first word of the sentence and add commas when necessary.

1. _____ The Healthy Lifestyle website provides accurate and useful nutrition advice
   (a)
   so/so that users feel better informed about issues related to health and exercise.
   (b)

2. _____ the site educates users about food and nutrition ___*so that*___ people can make
   (a)   (b)
   wise diet choices.

3. ___*So*___ users can keep track of their daily intake of calories, vitamins, and minerals
   (a)

   _____ the site includes nutrition charts on a wide variety of foods.
   (b)

4. _____ Healthy Lifestyle suggests that users get a physical exam ___*So that*___ they
   (a)   (b)
   know they are healthy enough to start a diet.

5. ___*So that*___ users will feel that their membership is a good deal _____ Healthy
   (a)   (b)
   Lifestyle publishes articles on a wide variety of topics.

6. _____ the site asks for personal information ___*so that*___ Healthy Lifestyle doctors
   (a)   (b)
   and nutritionists can design the best weight-loss program for each individual.

7. _____*so*_____ users will feel confident about the privacy of their information _____
   (a)   (b)

   Healthy Lifestyle publishes a privacy statement.

8. _____ Healthy Lifestyle provides downloadable calorie charts __*so that*__ users have
   (a)   (b)

   a reference to take to stores and restaurants.

2 Complete the sentences about the Paramount Medical Group. Use adverb clauses and
infinitives of purpose, and the correct form of the words in parentheses.

1. Medical practices use electronic communication and record-keeping processes

   in order to save time and money. (in order to; save)

2. The Paramount Medical Group answers health questions by e-mail _____

   patients come to the office unnecessarily. (so as to; not have)

3. The Paramount Medical Group sends appointment reminders by text message

   _____ so many phone calls. (in order to; not make)

4. Dr. Sands created a "Frequently Asked Questions" page for the practice's Web site

   _____ the number of phone calls he receives. (in order to; cut down on)

5. Dr. Yee sent his office staff to a seminar _____ their computer skills.

   (in order to; improve)

6. Dr. Ramirez's patients e-mail her with their symptoms before the appointment

   _____ consultation time more efficiently. (so as to; use)

7. The physician's assistant researches medications online _____ accurate and

   up-to-date prescription information to patients. (in order to; give)

8. All medical records at the Paramount Medical Group are electronic _____

   paper. (so as to; not waste)

9. The Paramount Medical Group has implemented a new record-keeping system

   _____ important patient information. (in order to; not lose)

3 A Complete the sentences about physicians. Circle the words that correctly complete each sentence.

1. What do doctors need to learn **to** / **so that** communicate with patients from different backgrounds?

2. As surprising as it may seem, some doctors do not understand that they need to smile **to** / **so that** put patients at ease.

3. **To** / **So that** they can better treat patients, many physicians require training in behavior that acknowledges the patient's feelings and background, called "bedside manner."

4. For example, medical schools offer courses in bedside manner **to** / **so that** physicians will be more sensitive to patients' needs.

5. They offer training in reading facial expressions and body language **to** / **so that** physicians can better interpret patients' feelings.

6. Many physicians also need to understand cultural differences in medicine and health **in order to** / **so that** treat patients from different cultures.

7. For example, many physicians forget not **to** / **so that** make eye contact with patients from certain cultures.

8. **To** / **So that** help with this, the Centers for Disease Control (CDC) publishes a series of pamphlets on cross-cultural communication.

9. The pamphlets include topics such as eye contact and touching in several cultures **to** / **so that** physicians will be aware of the cultural issues that they need to understand.

B Read the sentences in A again. Then answer the question.

Which sentences in A are examples of repetitive use of *to*? _____ On a separate piece of paper, rewrite the sentences to avoid repetition.

Reducing Adverb Clauses to Phrases

1 Rewrite the words in bold as reduced adverb clauses.

1. **When they are looking** for a new doctor, many people start their search online.

   When looking for a new doctor, many people start their search online.

2. **Before you start** to search online, read these tips.

   _____ to search online, read these tips.

3. **Before you go** online, decide if you are looking for a specialist or a general practitioner.

   _____ online, decide if you are looking for a specialist or a general practitioner.

4. **Before you look**, decide how important the doctor's gender, age, and location are.

   _____ , decide how important the doctor's gender, age, and location are.

5. **While you are searching**, notice the physician's specialty, where he or she attended medical school, and how long he or she has been practicing.

   _____ , notice the physician's specialty, where he or she attended medical school, and how long he or she has been practicing.

6. **While you are studying** the information that you find online, keep in mind that there is a great deal of inaccurate information on the Internet.

   _____ the information that you find online, keep in mind that there is a great deal of inaccurate information on the Internet.

7. **When they are researching** physicians online, many people visit doctor-rating sites.

   _____ physicians online, many people visit doctor-rating sites.

8. **When you are reading** doctor-rating sites, remember that you are reading people's opinions, and not facts.

   _____ doctor-rating sites, remember that you are reading people's opinions, and not facts.

9. **After they do** research online, many people consult social media websites to get further information about the doctor they have chosen.

   _____ research online, many people consult social media websites to get further information about the doctor they have chosen.

10. A study showed that **after they found** a doctor online using social media sites, most people were happy with their choice.

    A study showed that _____ a doctor online using social media sites, most people were happy with their choice.

2 Rewrite the words in bold as reduced adverb clauses.

1. **After she had suffered** for several weeks, the patient finally decided to get help.

   Having suffered for several weeks, the patient finally decided to get help.

2. **After she had had** a bad experience with a doctor in the past, the patient was hesitant to see a physician about her problem.

   _____ a bad experience with a doctor in the past, the patient was hesitant to see a physician about her problem.

3. **After she had consulted** a physician who could not help her, she wasn't sure any doctor could help.

   _____ a physician who could not help her, she wasn't sure any doctor could help.

4. **After she had spoken** with her friends about her condition, she finally decided to see a new doctor.

   _____ with her friends about her condition, she finally decided to see a new doctor.

5. **After she had received** doctor recommendations from several friends, she was ready to choose a new physician.

   _____ doctor recommendations from several friends, she was ready to choose a new physician.

6. **After she had found** a new doctor, she finally made an appointment.

   _____ a new doctor, she finally made an appointment.

3 Write sentences about an experience you had finding a doctor. Use reduced adverb clauses with *when*, *while*, *before*, and *after*.

1. *While searching for a new doctor, I visited several websites that rate doctors.*

2. _____

   _____

3. _____

   _____

4. _____

   _____

Common Vocabulary to Describe Problems and Solutions

1 Complete the sentences about fighting fatigue. Use the words in the box. Sometimes more than one answer is possible, and you will use some words more than once.

by	for	of	to	in

There are several ways _to_ address the problem ___of___ (2) fatigue. The solution ___to___ (3) the problem lies ___in___ (4) the patients themselves. One solution ___to___ (5) fatigue would be to get more exercise. The problem ___of___ (6) fatigue can also often be solved ___by___ (7) changes in diet. Medication is another possible solution ___to___ (8) the problem ___of___ (9) fatigue.

considered	necessary

In some cases of extreme fatigue, certain medical conditions must be ___considered___ (10). Medication may be ___considered___ (11) if the patient has a hormonal condition such as a malfunctioning thyroid. Major lifestyle changes should be ___considered___ (12) for many patients suffering from fatigue. Psychotherapy is ___necessary___ (13) in some cases of fatigue.

secondary	possible	primary

Reduced functioning in a patient's personal life is the ___primary___ (14) issue with fatigue. However, a ___secondary___ (15) issue is poor work performance. When people experience fatigue, they are likely to perform poorly at work. Fatigue may stem from an overtiring job itself. A ___possible___ (16) solution to this problem is for the patient to reconsider his or her work situation. A reduced workload may have very positive effects on a patient's body and mind.

2 Complete the sentences about Internet addiction. Write the correct form of the verbs in parentheses.

1. There *are* several ways to *address* the problem of Internet addiction. (address, be)

2. One solution to Internet addiction _____is_____ to _____limit_____ the number of hours you _____ online. (be, spend, limit)

3. Another solution _____is_____ to _____move_____ your computer to an uncomfortable location, such as the garage. (move, be)

4. The problem of Internet addiction can often _____ by having a friend or relative _____ your use. (solve, monitor)

5. If the problem of Internet addiction _____become_____ severe, therapy _____is_____ a possible solution. (be, become)

6. An exercise program _____ for many people who _____suffer_____ from Internet addiction. (consider, suffer)

3 On a separate piece of paper, write three sentences making recommendations of possible solutions. Use the problems in the list and the phrases in the box.

is needed/necessary	should be considered
might/may be considered	must be considered

Problems

cyberchondria

inaccurate information on the Internet

the high cost of medical care

your own ideas

The fact that you may come across inaccurate information should be

considered before taking the advice on websites.

Avoid Common Mistakes

1 Circle the mistakes.

1. Some physicians do not want their patients **to feel** anxious (**so that**) they **give** them a list
                                             (a)   (b)   (c)
   of medical websites.

2. **The** problem of **the** hypochondria can sometimes **be** solved with medication.
     (a)   (b)   (c)

3. Many physical problems can **be caused** by anxiety. **For examples,** headaches
   (a)   (b)   (c)
   and fatigue.

4. One can **find** reliable **information** on certain sites; **for examples,** sites with URLs
   (a)   (b)   (c)
   ending in ".gov" or ".edu."

5. Many physicians want **to spend** their consultation time more efficiently **so that** they
   (a)   (b)
   use e-mail to communicate with patients.
   (c)

6. **The** problem of **the** cyberchondria is **a result of** patients having too much access
   (a)   (b)   (c)
   to information.

7. **The** problem of **the** Internet addiction did not **exist** 30 years ago.
   (a)   (b)   (c)

8. The patient **wasn't able** to reduce his Internet use on his own, **so that** he started
   (a)   (b)
   therapy **to fight** his addiction.
   (c)

2 Identify the common mistakes in the sentences. Label each sentence with the type of
mistake from the box. If there is no mistake, write *d*. Then correct each sentence.

> a. Remember that *for example* is always singular, even when several examples follow.
> b. Remember that the phrase *The problem of* is not followed by *the*.
> c. Remember not to confuse *so that* (to express purpose) and *so* (to express result).
> d. There is no mistake.

b There are many solutions to the problem of ~~the~~ anxiety. *a* For examples,
(1)   (2)
removing the causes of stress in one's life and making small lifestyle changes can greatly
help anxiety sufferers. *c* The first step is to try to identify the causes of anxiety so the
(3)
individual can determine whether they can be eliminated. *a* For examples, unpleasant
(4)
working conditions and not having enough money are two common causes of stress. *d*
(5)
While individuals may not be able to quit their jobs, counseling may help anxiety sufferers,
giving them strategies so they can cope better with difficult situations. *c* People
(6)
with financial problems can learn money-management techniques so they eliminate
that particular source of stress. *b* The problem of the anxiety can also be solved by
(7)
changing one's lifestyle. *a* For examples, regular exercise and a healthy diet can help
(8)
eliminate stress. *c* Exercise is often relaxing, so that it alleviates stress. *a* Avoiding
(9)   (10)
certain foods and drinks that may lead to anxiety, for examples, caffeinated beverages and
sugary foods, can also help reduce anxiety.

Self-Assessment

Circle the word or phrase that correctly completes each sentence.

1. The students are learning how to evaluate websites __c__ they can avoid inaccurate information.

   a. so as to   b. to   c. so

2. Some people look at medical websites __a__ to be better informed.

   a. in order   b. so that   c. so

3. __b__ use consultation time more efficiently, some doctors have their patients fill out forms online.

   a. So   b. In order to   c. So that

4. The patient didn't want to spend a lot of time at the doctor's office, __c__ she made a list of questions before the appointment.

   a. so as to   b. so that   c. so

5. The doctor learned Spanish __a__ communicate better with some of her patients.

   a. to   b. so that   c. so

6. __b__ that they can understand their patients better, many physicians study "bedside manner."

   a. To   b. So   c. In order to

7. Before __a__ online, decide what you are looking for.

   a. going   b. to go   c. you are going

8. While __c__ for a new doctor, she consulted many doctor-rating websites.

   a. to look   b. look   c. looking

9. Having __a__ many people, she finally found a new physician.

   a. seen   b. seeing   c. see

10. Having __b__ the symptoms online, she began to worry.

    a. find   b. found   c. finding

11. One solution __b__ the problem of obesity is to increase the number of physical education classes in the schools.

    a. by   b. to   c. of

12. The high cost of medical care must __b__ .

    a. be needed   b. be considered   c. consider

13. If a cold or the flu lasts for several days, __c__ to see a doctor.

    a. necessary   b. it is needed   c. it may be necessary

14. There are many solutions to __a__ cyberchondria.

    a. the problem of   b. the problem   c. the problem of the

15. There are many signs of cyberchondria. __b__ , a patient may be anxious or argumentative.

    a. An example   b. For example   c. For examples

It Constructions

1 Unscramble the sentences about diet and exercise from a health class.

1. to / it / extend / by choosing healthier foods / your life / possible / may be

   It may be possible to extend your life by choosing healthier foods.

2. it / to / might be / your diet / difficult / change

   _____

3. might not work / is / that / possible / a diet / it

   _____

4. too much / be / exercise / may not / helpful / it / to do

   _____

5. are / it / that / seems / the first weeks of a diet / very difficult

   _____

6. be / some foods / it / our memories / might / true / that / strengthen

   _____

7. that / enough nutrients / it / is / do not provide / true / some vegetables

   _____

8. appears / energy levels / healthy eating / that / it / improves

   _____

9. that people should eat / five servings of fruit and vegetables a day / it seems

   _____

2 Complete the sentences about herbal remedies. Use *that*, *to*, or *for*.

1. It is possible *to* treat some illnesses with herbs.

2. It is sometimes difficult _____ people to find natural herbs in stores.

3. It is likely _____ some herbal remedies are from ancient times.

4. It is easy _____ forget that some herbs are poisonous.

5. It is true _____ some doctors don't approve of herbal remedies.

6. It seems _____ some people trust herbal remedies more than antibiotics.

7. It is hard _____ some people to accept herbal remedies as legitimate medicine.

8. It is difficult _____ prepare some herbal medicines at home.

9. It is essential _____ research herbal medicines before taking them.

10. It is important _____ follow the directions on the packaging.

11. It is unlikely _____ herbal medicine will replace conventional medicine.

12. It is evident _____ some herbs are effective in treating certain ailments.

3 Complete the sentences about the benefits of vitamins using *it* constructions. Use an infinitive or *that* clause and the word in parentheses.

1. *It is important to* boost your immune system with Vitamin C. (important)

2. _____ Vitamin A prevents or decreases flu symptoms. (appear)

3. _____ absorb Vitamin D in the winter. (difficult)

4. _____ people will get the flu in the summer months. (unlikely)

5. _____ Vitamin B6 helps the nervous system. (seem)

6. _____ people seek advice from their doctor before taking new vitamins. (best)

7. _____ prevent anemia by taking iron. (possible)

8. _____ Vitamin K interacts badly with some medicines. (appear)

9. _____ some vitamins taken in the correct dosage are beneficial. (certain)

10. _____ boost your immune system by eating properly and getting lots of sleep. (easy)

11. _____ regular exercise makes people feel healthier and happier. (true)

12. _____ people should limit the amount of junk food they consume. (obvious)

4 Rewrite the sentences. Use a passive voice *it* construction for the words in bold.

1. **Researchers have found** that vegetarians often lack sufficient iron in their diets.

   It has been found that vegetarians often lack sufficient iron in their diets.

2. **Doctors suggest** that people with allergies to dairy products drink soy milk.

   _____ that people with allergies to dairy products drink soy milk.

3. **People believe** that diets high in sugar and fat are very unhealthy.

   _____ that diets high in sugar and fat are very unhealthy.

4. **Doctors have proven** that diets high in fiber are good for the digestive system.

   _____ that diets high in fiber are good for the digestive system.

5. **Researchers can show** that artificial sweeteners have negative effects on animals.

   _____ that artificial sweeteners have negative effects on animals.

6. **Doctors have found** that patients who followed vegan diets had healthy hearts.

   _____ that patients who followed vegan diets had healthy hearts.

7. **People think** that gluten-free diets are difficult to follow.

   _____ that gluten-free diets are difficult to follow.

8. **People accept** that some people follow strictly vegetarian diets.

   _____ that some people follow strictly vegetarian diets.

9. **Scientists have found** that certain vegetables and fruits have anticancer properties.

   _____ that certain vegetables and fruits have anticancer properties.

5 Complete the sentences. Write about healthy eating habits. Use your own ideas.

1. It may be true that *vitamins are good for you, but I think they should be taken in moderation* .

2. It could be argued that _____ .

3. It might seem that _____ .

4. It's important to _____ .

5. It's essential to _____ .

Common Transition Words to Indicate Steps of a Solution

1 Read the web article about the treatment of dehydration in the body. Then label the purpose of each word or phrase in bold.

A = to introduce the first step	C = to indicate steps happening at the same time
B = to introduce additional steps	D = to conclude the process

Living Without **Water**

Dehydration is a very serious issue around the world for children, athletes, and others who may be susceptible to it. _A_ **First**, there has to be a reason for the process to begin,
(1)
whether it is an illness causing loss of fluids, or extreme physical activity in hot weather.

_____ **At the same time**, the lost fluid is not being replaced at all, or is not being replaced
(2)
quickly enough. Dehydration _____ **then** continues, and physical signs become obvious.
(3)

What physical signs are evident during the process of dehydration? _____ **To begin**,
(4)
the person may get a headache, or the face may turn red. _____ **After that**, the symptoms
(5)
may become more unusual, for example an inability to drink, or crying with no tears.

_____ **Following that**, the symptoms become more severe, including fainting, extreme
(6)
muscle cramping, or rapid heart rate. _____ **Last**, the person may go into shock, which is a
(7)
serious medical condition. The person could die from shock.

As soon as these more severe symptoms appear, it is extremely important to
seek urgent medical care and monitor the person as he or she receive fluids.

2 Read the informational flier about the process of finding a personal trainer. Complete the sentences with a word or phrase from the box. Capitalize the first word of the sentence when necessary.

after that	second	third	Ø
last	then	~~to begin~~	

In their efforts to get fit, many people seek help from a personal trainer, but finding a personal trainer can be difficult. In order to find a good trainer, consider using a systematic approach. _To begin_ , ask family and friends for recommendations. If this
(1)
fails, ask for a recommendation at a local gym. _____ , schedule an appointment
(2)
just to meet the trainer, not to begin training. _____ , interview the trainer about
(3)
the training programs he or she uses, including types of exercises, diets, and any other parts of the training program. If the trainer seems like a good match, you should _____ ask about his or her education and certification. _____ It is very
(4) (5)
important that you choose someone who has been educated and licensed to train you. _____ , you will want to discuss specific details of your program, including
(6)
rates, and develop a detailed program, together with your trainer, that you can follow. _____ , begin your program and find a healthier you!
(7)

3 Read the sentences about choosing a doctor. Write a paragraph on the next page using the sentences with transition words to indicate the process.

1. Decide whether you prefer a male or a female doctor.

2. Ask friends and family for recommendations.

3. Contact the doctors' offices to find out about their hours, rates, and the insurance plans they accept.

4. Make a list of questions to ask the doctors.

5. Make an appointment to interview the doctors and then ask your questions.

6. Choose a doctor based on the interviews.

7. If you already have a doctor, notify him or her that you would like to have your records forwarded to the new doctor.

_____

_____

_____

_____

_____

_____

_____

_____

_____

Avoid Common Mistakes

1 Circle the mistakes.

1. **It is important** **to** monitor calorie intake. First list the foods you eat. **Than** estimate
       (a)   (b)   (c)
   how much you eat.

2. **It is impossible Ø** underestimate the effects of first overeating and **then** failing
       (a)   (b)   (c)
   to exercise.

3. **It is importand to** first talk to your doctor. **Then** you can start a diet you agree on.
       (a)   (b)   (c)

4. **It is often impossible convince** some people that **it is important** **to** exercise.
       (a)   (b)   (c)

5. **It is important** **to** see a doctor once a year, and **it is also import** to go to the dentist.
       (a)   (b)   (c)

6. As we age, our hearing may deteriorate first and **then** our eyesight, but **it's impossible**
                            (a)   (b)
   Ø us to predict how severe the loss will be.
   (c)

7. **It is important** **to** see a doctor, but it may be impossible **Ø** convince sick people to
       (a)   (b)   (c)
   do so.

8. **It is important** **to** schedule your day well and **than** get enough sleep at night.
       (a)   (b)   (c)

2 Identify the common mistakes in the sentences. Label each sentence with the type of mistake from the box. If there is no mistake, write *d*. Then correct each sentence.

> a. Remember to use *It is important to* and not *It is import to* or *It is importand to*.
> b. Remember to use *to* or *for* after *impossible*.
> c. Remember to use *then*, and not *than*, when introducing next steps.
> d. There is no mistake.

important

_a_ According to a research study at a major American university, it is very ~~import~~
(1)

to have a good attitude in order to stay healthy. _____ For many people, it is impossible
(2)

believe that our attitudes can affect our health, but this seems to be true. _____ Most
(3)

people understand that it is importand to be positive in order to be happy. _____
(4)

According to researchers, a positive attitude first lowers blood pressure and than other

positive effects follow, such as healthier blood flow and heart rate. _____ These findings are
(5)

noteworthy because it is important to remember that heart health has a strong influence

on overall health. _____ Although it is impossible researchers to measure exactly how
(6)

much a positive attitude can benefit the heart, it is definitely significant. _____ So, the next
(7)

time you are feeling upset, remind yourself of the results of this study, than take a deep

breath and try to relax.

Self-Assessment

Circle the word or phrase that correctly completes each sentence.

1. It is difficult _____ some people to discuss their health problems with others.

    a. to   b. for   c. that

2. It _____ that the portion sizes in American restaurants are too large.

    a. suggest   b. suggested   c. has been suggested

3. _____ , the nurse will take your temperature. Then he will check your blood pressure.

    a. To begin   b. Last   c. Third

4. It is impossible _____ know how long someone will live.

    a. to   b. for   c. that

5. It is not recommended _____ chicken at a dinner that vegetarians will attend.

    a. serving   b. to serve   c. serve

6. If you are in an accident, first make sure you are all right. You can _____ get out of the car if it is safe to do so.

   a. after that   b. last   c. then

7. When dieting, it is helpful to write what you ate as soon as you are finished eating. _____ , make a note of any items that you can eliminate next time to cut calories.

   a. At the same time   b. As soon as   c. First

8. It is advisable _____ you go to the hospital if you get a serious burn.

   a. to   b. for   c. that

9. When storing fresh food, first choose a container, then put the food in and close it immediately. _____ , store the container in the refrigerator.

   a. Than   b. To begin   c. Finally

10. It _____ that women who felt comfortable with their doctors had fewer health problems.

    a. were found   b. was found   c. found

11. It is useful _____ the phone numbers of your dentist and doctor in your phone's contact list.

    a. to keep   b. keeping   c. kept

12. During an emergency, _____ call for an ambulance. Then attend to any people who are hurt.

    a. following that   b. first   c. last

13. It may be possible _____ a long time even with very advanced cancer.

    a. to live   b. that lived   c. have lived

14. It is often difficult _____ poor people to afford fresh fruits and vegetables.

    a. to   b. for   c. that

15. To lose weight, first talk to your doctor. _____ , you should follow the doctor's instructions.

    a. In the end   b. After that   c. Third

Summary–Response

Privacy in the Digital Age

Past Unreal Conditionals

1 Complete the sentences about using computers at work. Write the correct form of the verbs in parentheses. Use past unreal conditionals.

1. If *you hadn't used* (not / use) the computer to play games, your manager *wouldn't*

   have been (not / be) upset.

2. Your computer _____ (be) safe from attack if you _____ (sign) out.

3. If you _____ (not / open) that file, a virus _____ (not / infect)

   the network.

4. The network security team _____ (not / contact) you if you

   _____ (not / report) that virus.

5. If you _____ (not / spend) so much time reading blogs, you

   _____ (finish) your report.

6. If you _____ (close) your personal e-mail, your manager

   _____ (not / see) it.

2 Circle the sentence that expresses true information about the past unreal conditional statement.

1. If she had used a surge protector, she wouldn't have damaged her computer.

   a. Her computer is fine.

   b. Her computer is damaged.

   c. She used a surge protector.

2. Blanca wouldn't have been a victim of identity theft if she had not entered her credit card information on a strange website.

   a. Blanca was a victim of identity theft.

   b. Blanca didn't enter information on a strange website.

   c. Blanca was not a victim of identity theft.

3. His laptop wouldn't have broken if it had been in a case.

    a. His laptop was in a case.

    b. His laptop fell out of a case.

    c. His laptop broke.

4. If Joe had used only one credit card online, thieves wouldn't have gotten the numbers of all three of his credit cards.

    a. Joe only had one credit card.

    b. Joe only used one credit card online.

    c. Joe used more than one credit card online.

5. If Mary had used a stronger password, hackers might not have been able to figure it out.

    a. Hackers weren't able to figure out Mary's password.

    b. Mary didn't use a strong password.

    c. Mary told hackers her password.

6. If Tina had logged out of her account, other people wouldn't have been able to use it.

    a. Tina didn't log out of her account.

    b. Others weren't able to use Tina's account.

    c. Tina logged out of her account.

7. If Luis had charged his laptop, it wouldn't have shut down while he was making a purchase.

    a. The computer didn't shut down.

    b. The computer was charged.

    c. The computer wasn't charged.

8. If Akiko had had a Wi-Fi connection, she could have been able to send the report.

    a. Akiko didn't have a Wi-Fi connection.

    b. Akiko sent the report.

    c. Akiko had a Wi-Fi connection.

9. If Pietro hadn't forgotten his username, he could have bought the tickets he wants online.

   a. Pietro didn't forget his username.

   b. Pietro bought the tickets online.

   c. Pietro forgot his username.

10. If I had bought a smartphone, I wouldn't have needed to take a laptop on my trip.

   a. I bought a smartphone.

   b. I didn't buy a smartphone.

   c. I didn't bring a laptop.

3 Unscramble the sentences about privacy and technology. Add commas when necessary.

1. If / we would have responded / they had texted us

   If they had texted us, we would have responded.

2. If / your number / I had recognized / the phone / I would have answered

   _____

3. you wouldn't have gotten / you had visited / only trusted websites / the computer virus / If

   _____

4. Murat hadn't given his number to strangers / he wouldn't have received / If / prank phone calls

   _____

5. on strange links / If / you wouldn't have had problems / you hadn't clicked

   _____

6. I would have received / your e-mail / If / I had logged on

   _____

7. if / You couldn't have / protected your password very well / your e-mail was hacked

   _____

8. online / the money / used your credit card / if you hadn't / you wouldn't have lost

   _____

9. had been more patient / If / your laptop / wouldn't have crashed / you

_____

10. the news report online / we wouldn't have known / If / about the scam / we hadn't seen

_____

4 Complete the sentences about technology. Write sentences that are true for you. Use past unreal conditionals.

1. If the Internet had never been invented, _I would have spent more money on_

   stamps last year .

2. If cell phones had never been developed, _____

   _____ .

3. If I hadn't learned how to use a computer, _____

   _____ .

4. If social media hadn't been created, _____

   _____ .

5. If e-mail hadn't existed, _____

   _____ .

Common Phrases Used in Summary–Response Writing

1 Read Ingrid's summary–response paper about an article on safely using a public Wi-Fi network. Underline the phrases of summary–response writing. Then label each phrase.

> A = introduces and identifies the ideas of the original text
> B = indicates what the author omitted or did not consider
> C = concludes the summary

_A_ <u>The article</u> "Protecting Yourself in Public" <u>provides</u> valuable information on
(1)

how to protect important personal information when using public Wi-Fi networks.

_____ According to the author, Wi-Fi networks in libraries, coffee shops, and airports
(2)

are convenient, but can be dangerous because others may have an easier time

accessing sensitive information. _____ The author further explains that it is often the
(3)

actions of the victim that lead the individual to become a victim. _____ The author
(4)

goes on to show how people don't realize that when checking their e-mail, their

password may be observed, making it possible for others to access the account. _____
(5)

The author concludes that using only secure computers for things such as online

shopping and banking is the only way to protect oneself.

_____ The author fails to address the fact that, for economic reasons, many people
(6)

do not have access to a secure computer. _____ The author does not mention that, for
(7)

some individuals, their work schedules are such that they have to do business in an

airport. _____ Furthermore, the author fails to provide useful advice for those who are
(8)

most likely to be harmed by such actions.

2 Read the beginning of Daniel's summary–response paper on an article about identifying fraudulent e-mails. Write the word or phrase from the box that best completes each sentence. Sometimes more than one answer may be possible.

~~addresses~~	starts	concludes	goes on to give
also says	states	fails to address	summing up

Emily Black, the director of the Online Consumer Protection Foundation,

addresses the issue of fraudulent e-mails and how to identify them in an article
(1)

entitled "More Than a Simple Request" (2011). She _____ her article
(2)

by explaining that thousands of people fall victim to online scams involving e-mail.

She _____ that there are ways that consumers can recognize fraudulent
(3)

e-mails and protect themselves from them. She _____ several examples
(4)

of ways to recognize these e-mails, including looking for spelling errors and odd

return e-mail addresses. The article _____ when people should inform law
(5)

enforcement about fraudulent e-mails. Black _____ the article with a list
(6)

of agencies that counsel consumers who have been harmed by fraudulent e-mails.

_____ , this article is helpful, but it did not go far enough. For example, the
(7)

author _____ some of the most common tricks that criminals use to gain
(8)

access to passwords, such as launching spyware through seemingly innocent links.

3 Read an article or text of your choice. On a separate piece of paper, summarize it using
the summary–response phrases from Ingrid and Daniel's essays. Then respond using
appropriate phrases to express agreement or disagreement.

Avoid Common Mistakes

1 Circle the mistakes.

1. If you **hadn't left** your password on your desk, people wouldn't have (saw) it.
       (a)   (b)   (c)
2. We wouldn't **have experience** a security breach if you hadn't **used** personal e-mail.
                (a)   (b)   (c)
3. The author **starts out** with a **list** of all the security **pitfalls** many people fall into.
              (a)   (b)   (c)
4. She **looks into** the process of **recovering** an identity once it's been **stolen**.
        (a)   (b)   (c)
5. She **expects** the reader to **put up with** a lot of ambiguity about **network** safety.
       (a)   (b)   (c)
6. I would not have **wrote** to your work e-mail if you had **told** me it had been **hacked**.
             (a)   (b)   (c)
7. If we had **known** there **was** a virus, we would have **took** further precautions.
        (a)   (b)   (c)
8. The article **addresses** the difficulty of **finding out** where security breaches **originate**.
     (a)   (b)   (c)

2 Identify the common mistakes in the sentences. Label each sentence with the type of mistake from the box. If there is no mistake, write *c*. Then correct each sentence.

> a. Remember to use the past participle form of the verb after the modal in past unreal conditional sentences.
>
> b. Remember to use academic, precise words rather than multi-word verbs or idioms.
>
> c. There is no mistake.

_b_ (1) In her article on how companies use social media in the hiring process, Sarah Valero-Preston ~~looks into~~ *investigates* the ethical issues as well as the practical ones of such investigations. _____ (2) Valero-Preston starts out with a description of the things that companies are concerned about. _____ (3) She then explains how companies use investigators to search for relevant information about the job applicants. _____ (4) If many job seekers had understood how their personal comments on blogs could hurt them, they probably would have took more time in choosing their words. _____ (5) According to the author, the job seekers must consent to the process before anyone can look into their social media history. _____ (6) Of course, the investigators start out with the popular social media sites, but they also search even deeper for comments on these sites and less well-known ones. _____ (7) If some applicants had known about such extensive searches, Valero-Preston wonders if they would have consented. _____ (8) The author wraps up by reminding us that the Internet is a public space, and anyone can search your name.

Self-Assessment

Circle the word or phrase that correctly completes each sentence.

1. If you hadn't made those comments on social media sites, the company would have _____ you.

   a. hire   b. hired   c. hiring

2. I'm not certain, but you _____ have been able to stop the investigation if you had confessed.

   a. might   b. would   c. couldn't

3. The authors _____ the article by making recommendations for further research in the field.

   a. wrap up   b. conclude   c. further state

4. The author has failed to _____ the realities of using social media at work.

   a. address   b. not mention   c. start

5. If we _____ the document, we would not have lost so much data.

   a. save   b. saved   c. had saved

6. The investigators would not have _____ your comments if you had used a different username.

   a. find   b. found   c. founded

7. _____ the author, social media sites are not always as private as we think.

   a. Summing up   b. Discussing   c. According to

8. Many people would not _____ having their Internet history searched in order to secure a job.

   a. put up with   b. tolerate   c. stand for

9. The company would not _____ any evidence to fire you if you hadn't used your work e-mail.

   a. have had   b. had had   c. have been having

10. _____ , the author didn't prove that networks are more secure today than they were last year.

   a. According to   b. In conclusion   c. Wrapping up

11. If we _____ our password, hackers would have continued using our account.

   a. hadn't changed   b. had changed   c. changed

12. The author _____ that online banking is very safe. He then discusses the merits of it.

   a. sums up   b. quotes   c. further states

13. If you hadn't explained the security process to me, I wouldn't have _____ .

   a. understand   b. understood   c. understanding

14. The author _____ the subject in depth.

   a. notes that   b. goes on to explain   c. concludes that

15. If I _____ my phone, I would have texted you sooner.

   a. hadn't lost   b. was lost   c. didn't lose

Nonidentifying Relative Clauses in Persuasive Writing

1 Underline the relative clauses in the sentences about violence in the media. Then label each sentence. Add commas when necessary.

> NI = nonidentifying   I = identifying

1. _NI_ Our sociology professor, <u>who is also the father of three</u>, believes that violence in movies has created a less sensitive population.

2. _NI_ According to our professor, violent movies, which are quite popular today, have not had positive effects on many children.

3. _NI_ Our class spoke to Dr. Samantha Smith, who is a psychology professor, about the effects of movie violence on teenagers.

4. _I_ Dr. Smith says that violence which is portrayed as funny is particularly offensive to parents.

5. _I_ She reports that many children, who are younger than 17 regularly see violent movies with older siblings or friends.

6. _NI_ Dr. Smith's children who are both between the ages of 6 and 10, are not permitted to watch violent movies.

7. _NI_ Dr. Henry Brown, whose mother is also a researcher, is known for conducting studies about the effect of violence on children.

8. _I_ Dr. Brown has found that movies which show women and children in frightening situations are extremely disturbing to many people.

2 Complete the sentences about Olga's brothers. Use *whose, who, which,* or *Ø.* Then label each clause *NI* (for nonidentifying adjective clause) or *A* (for appositive).

1. _NI_ My parents have activated the parental controls on our only television, _which_ is located in the living room.

2. _Ø_ My aunt, _____ a parent of three boys, feels strongly about preventing her children from watching violent television shows.

3. _NI_ My aunt's best friend, _whose_ child is permitted to watch anything, is not nearly so strict about violent television shows.

4. _NI_ My brothers, _who_ are always trying to turn off the parental controls, often argue with my parents about television shows.

5. _NI_ Their favorite shows, _whose_ names I can't recall, are sometimes violent.

6. _Ø_ Sometimes my brothers visit Kevin, _____ the son of my aunt's friend, when they want to watch TV.

7. _NI_ My parents' opinions, _which_ do not seem to matter to my brothers, aren't enough to change their behavior.

8. _NI_ My opinion, _which_ is the same as my aunt's, is that my parents should not permit my brothers to go to Kevin's house.

3 Complete the blog post about Bryant's child psychology professors. Use the appropriate clause from the box.

a child advocacy organization	a very popular children's television show
all psychology majors	located in the center of campus
~~an expert on child psychology~~	work appears in many respected journals
difficult to write	writes extensively on child psychology

Semester Update 1

I am enjoying my semester so far. Alex Mason is my professor. Professor Mason, who

is _an expert on child psychology_ , has written two books on the effects of television
    (1)

on children. You can get a copy of her book at the university's psychology research

center, which is _located in the center of campus_ . Dr. Victoria Holcomb,
    (2)

who _writes extensively..._ , is also a professor at this university.
    (3)

Professor Holcomb, whose _work appears..._ , often conducts
    (4)

joint research with Professor Mason. The Foundation for Child Safety, which is

a child advocacy... , has funded much of their research on the
    (5)

effects of violence on children. Last semester, Professors Mason and Holcomb conducted

research on *Action Heroes and Villains*, which is _a very popular..._ .
    (6)

My classmates and I, who are _all psychology majors_ , helped them write
    (7)

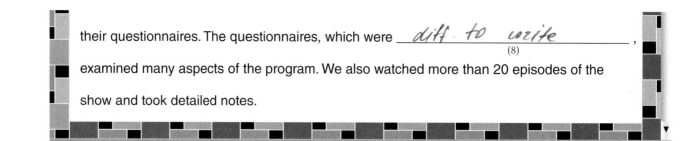

their questionnaires. The questionnaires, which were _diff. to write_ (8) ,
examined many aspects of the program. We also watched more than 20 episodes of the
show and took detailed notes.

4 Read the press release. Then write new sentences by adding the additional information,
using nonidentifying relative clauses.

1. Families United Against Violence has organized a conference for youth.
   Additional information: Families United Against Violence is a local nonprofit group.

   Families United Against Violence, which is a local nonprofit group, has
   organized a conference for youth.

2. Dr. Susan Smith will be giving a lecture on media violence at this conference.
   Additional information: Dr. Susan Smith's research is groundbreaking.

   Dr. Susan Smith, whose research is groundbreaking, will be...

3. *Captain Hero* is going to stop creating violent story lines.
   Additional information: Captain Hero is a popular children's show.

   Captain Hero, which is a popular children's show, is...

4. Nick Robinson is presenting a series of interviews from the conference.
   Additional information: Nick Robinson is a nationally recognized reporter.

   Nick Robinson, who is a nationally..., is presenting...

5. Theresa Filmore will be speaking at the conference.
   Additional information: Theresa Filmore is an award-winning journalist.

   Theresa Filmore, who is an award-winning..., will be...

6. *Time* will probably cover the conference.
   Additional information: Time is an American news magazine.

   Time, which is an American..., will probably...

7. Americans Against Violence organized a similar conference last year.
   Additional information: Americans Against Violence is a grassroots community group.

   AAV, which is a grassroots..., organized a similar...

8. Josh Willow has become president of this organization.
   Additional information: Josh Willow is a star high school athlete and scholar.

   Josh Willow, who is a star high..., has become...

Phrases That Limit Overgeneralization

1 Unscramble the sentences about violence in movies. Add punctuation when necessary.

1. young people / most violence in movies / to involve / tends

   Most violence in movies tends to involve young people.

2. are / watch / likely to / older people / dramatic or comedic movies

3. action movies / seems that / it / popular / are / with young people

4. the villain in a horror movie / people / to hate / tend

5. comedic movies / than violent movies / tend / more appealing / to be

6. appears that / is / it / the action movie / the best one in theaters now

7. seem / horror movies / weak plots and character development / to have

8. in most cases / roles in violent movies / avoid / my favorite actors

9. their fear of frightening movies / hide / typically / young teens

10. many reviewers / more critical of the acting in violent movies / tend / to be

11. appear / violent movies / shorter than nonviolent ones / to be

12. one news source / very worried / violence in popular movies / according to / about / parents are

2 Rewrite the sentences from a newspaper editorial. Use the expressions in parentheses to make them less generalized.

Have your say . . .

1. Teens who listen to heavy metal **are** more disrespectful to their parents and authority figures. (be likely to)

   Teens who listen to heavy metal _are likely to be_ more disrespectful to their parents and authority figures.

2. Heavy metal bands **attract** teens that have trouble with their parents. (tend to)

   Heavy metal bands _tend to attract_ teens that have trouble with their parents.

3. Teens who play music **cope** well with stress in their lives. (typically)

   Teens who play music _typically cope_ well with stress in their lives.

4. Violent lyrics in songs **have** a negative impact on teens. (mainly)

   Violent lyrics in songs _mainly have_ a negative impact on teens.

5. Parents who have positive relationships with their families **do not allow** their children to listen to music with violent lyrics. (appear not to)

   Parents who have positive relationships with their families _appear not to allow_ their children to listen to music with violent lyrics.

6. Violent music **is** louder and faster than nonviolent music. (be likely)

   Violent music _is likely to be_ louder and faster than nonviolent music.

7. Students who listen to violent music **are** less likely to have stable social lives. (seem to)

   Students who listen to violent music _seem to be_ less likely to have stable social lives.

8. Uplifting music **is** more popular with well-adjusted people. (appear to)

   Uplifting music _appears to be_ more popular with well-adjusted people.

9. Young people who listen to folk music or country music **do** well in school. (tend to)

   Young people who listen to folk music or country music _tend to do_ well in school.

Avoid Common Mistakes

1 Circle the mistakes.

1. It **seem** that afternoon cartoons, **which** strongly influence children, are in need of
(a) (b)
regulation. However, advertisers **that** sponsor kids' TV shows do not always agree.
(c)

2. Although a particular TV show may **seem** innocent, **it** may be a good idea for parents
(a) (b)
to watch it. They need to understand its influence, **that** may not be obvious, on
(c)
their children.

3. The articles from the *Herald-Sun*, **Ø** is the local newspaper, **seem** to be written by
(a) (b)
people with credentials **that** are very impressive.
(c)

4. Late-night television shows, **that** are intended for mature audiences, are the ones **that**
(a) (b)
usually scare me so much **that** I can't sleep.
(c)

5. My psychology professors **seem** to respect the research **that** was funded by the
(a) (b)
National Education Foundation, **Ø** is headquartered here.
(c)

6. It **seem** that the Society of Motion Picture Directors, **which** most movie directors
(a) (b)
belong to, believes that the degrees of violence in movies **seem** to be difficult to
(c)
define consistently.

7. The family-viewing hour, **Ø** is an hour of nonviolent television, **seems** to be unpopular
(a) (b)
with some people **who** are younger.
(c)

8. Advocates for a Violence-Free Society, **Ø** is a nonprofit organization, **seem** to be
(a) (b)
starting a campaign **that** asks senators to pass laws against media violence.
(c)

2 Identify the common mistakes in the sentences. Label each sentence with the type of mistake from the box. If there is no mistake, write *d*. Then correct each sentence.

> a. Remember to include the relative pronoun in nonidentifying relative clauses.
> b. Remember not to use *that* as a relative pronoun in nonidentifying relative clauses.
> c. Remember to use the singular form of the verb *seem* with *it*.
> d. There is no mistake.

> These days _c_ it ~~seem~~ *seems* that many parents are concerned about their children's favorite
> (1)
> TV shows _____. Some of these shows include violent images or events, *which* can have a huge
> (2)
> impression on young minds. _____ As a result, parents who are upset with the available
> (3)
> shows are taking matters into their own hands. _____ These parents use money, ~~that~~ *which* can
> (4)
> be a big motivator, to influence advertisers. _____ The angry parents do not simply write
> (5)
> e-mails and letters, *which* can easily be ignored or lost, but they stop buying those advertisers'
> products. _____ They also use social media to coordinate their campaigns, which makes
> (6)
> their efforts even more effective. _____ These parents have opponents, but it seem*s* that
> (7)
> momentum is on the side of the families.

Self-Assessment

Circle the word, phrase, or item that correctly completes each sentence.

1. The professor's interests, _____ are very complicated, are clearly outlined in this article.

   a. Ø   b. that   c. which

2. Violent movies _____ be released more frequently in the summer than in the winter.

   a. seems to   b. seem to   c. seems

3. Kevin Nelson, _____ an award-winning reporter, has recently written an article on violence in our community.

   a. which   b. Ø   c. who

4. Children who watch movies with a positive message _____ be more compassionate.

   a. tend to   b. tend   c. tends to

5. The senator, _____ voted for this bill just last month, is now completely opposed to it.

   a. which   b. who   c. that

6. Violent films, _____ content may affect kids, should be regulated.

   a. which   b. that   c. whose

7. My professor, _____ believes that violent films harm society, says they should be banned.

   a. who   b. whose   c. what

8. My brothers and I _____ to watch violent movies with large groups of friends.

   a. am likely   b. is likely   c. are likely

9. Parents for Safer Kids, _____ nonprofit organization, has begun a letter-writing campaign.

   a. a   b. Ø   c. which

10. It _____ unlikely that anyone can entirely avoid seeing violent television shows.

   a. seem   b. seems   c. Ø

11. _____ that violent movies really do have an influence on behavior.

   a. It seems   b. It's appears   c. It is

12. Stronger laws, _____ are worth discussing, might reduce violence in society.

   a. who   b. that   c. which

13. Tina James, _____ movie director, has made some of the most violent movies I've ever seen.

   a. a   b. which   c. Ø

14. The Concerned Parents Group, _____ encourages stricter media control, will protest today.

   a. Ø   b. which   c. that

15. A person's age and gender _____ have little influence on their preference for movie genres.

   a. appears to   b. appears   c. appear to

Persuasion 2

Living in an Age of Information Overload

Noun Clauses with *Wh-* Words and *If / Whether*

1 Complete the sentences about technology in the workplace. Circle the phrase that correctly completes each sentence.

1. Many employers, and many employees, are interested in _____ their workplaces more flexible.

   a. can modern technology make

   b. how can modern technology make

   c. how modern technology can make

2. Some employers are familiar with the old idea of teleworking, or working from home, but are unsure _____ .

   a. what should today's effective virtual workplace look like

   b. what today's effective virtual workplace should look like

   c. should today's effective virtual workplace look like

3. Forward-thinking companies are trying to decide _____ .

   a. how the wide range of new mobile technologies could benefit their employees

   b. how could the wide range of new mobile technologies benefit their employees

   c. the wide range of new mobile technologies could benefit their employees

4. Employers may not be sure _____ to keep their employees connected.

   a. which devices and equipment they need

   b. which devices and equipment do they need

   c. devices and equipment that they need

5. Employers also need to reflect on _____ , and then make sure their technology facilitates it.

   a. they want their employees to collaborate

   b. how do they want their employees to collaborate

   c. how they want their employees to collaborate

6. Experts will continue to debate _____ .

    a. type of workplace best for business

    b. which type of workplace is best for business

    c. type of workplace which is best for business

7. There is no general agreement on _____ .

    a. should communication technology be used in the workplace

    b. how should communication technology be used in the workplace

    c. how communication technology should be used in the workplace

8. However, because of the flexibility technology allows, employers should consider _____ .

    a. what they can do to take advantage of these exciting new tools

    b. what can they do to take advantage of these exciting new tools

    c. can they do to take advantage of these exciting new tools

2 Rewrite the questions about online courses. Use a noun clause with a *wh-* word to make statements.

1. How do online courses compare to traditional courses?

    Students today often wonder *how online courses compare to traditional courses* .

2. What types of learners are most likely to succeed in an online course?

    Students should look into _____ .

3. How successful are they at working independently?

    Students who are considering an online class should reflect on
    how successful they are at working independently .

4. What types of interactions with classmates do online students have?

    It is often not clear to potential online students _____ .

5. How much teacher time and attention do students receive?

    Before taking an online class, students should consider _how much teacher time and attention students receive._

6. How many courses are available online?

    It is not known _how many courses are available online_ .

7. Which institutions consider online courses the equivalent of traditional courses?

    It is not always clear _____ .

8. When might taking an online course lead to information overload?

Students should also consider _____.

9. How do successful online learners manage electronic distractions while they are trying to study?

Researchers are interested in _____.

3 Complete the sentences about how Andrew spends his time online. Match the phrases to correctly complete each sentence.

1. Andrew has been wondering whether _d_.

2. He often feels stressed, and he isn't sure _g_.

3. He's wondering if _a_.

4. He's asked himself _f_, he should just turn the computer off for the evening.

5. He is starting to focus on _c_ he spent less time online.

6. Andrew's wife is not sure if _b_.

7. She is wondering if Andrew _h_.

8. According to her, Andrew needs to start focusing _e_.

a. he would be happier if he limited his time online to a few hours a day

b. Andrew will really be able to make such a big change

c. whether his life would be more rewarding if

d. he is suffering from information overload.

e. on whether he is spending enough time with family and friends

f. whether every day at 7 p.m.

g. whether that stress is caused by the amount of time he spends online

h. might shut down the computer and then switch to checking social media sites on his phone

4 Complete the sentences about shopping for technology products. Write sentences that are true for you.

1. Before I buy any new technology, I think about _how useful it is going to be_.

2. Advertisements can be very persuasive, but I consider whether
   _____ how information it is truly _____.

3. Before people buy a new device, they should find out _when it has been produced_ and _how much it is cost_.

4. To decide whether I can trust an online information source, I always look at
   who is an author of this article.

5. Although I love gadgets, I always consider whether _how useful it is going to be for me_.

Phrases for Argumentation

1 Read the student essays. Label each sentence with the type of statement from the box.

savvy
здоровий глузд

OV = opposing view	R = refutation *спростування*	TS = thesis statement
AO = acknowledge an opposing argument	SI = supporting information	

визнавати

Student A

opinion

_TS_ (1) E-books should be used in elementary schools. _OV_ (2) It has been argued that traditional books are more connected to the "reading experience" for young children.

_AO_ (3) Obviously, traditional books are more economical for large school systems. _R_ (4) However, it is important for young students to be familiar with and able to use up-to-date technologies. _SI_ (5) Children who learn to use advanced technologies when they are young will have a big advantage when they are older.

Student B

_TS_ (6) The most important thing teachers can do in the elementary classroom is to spend time interacting with their students. _OV_ (7) It could be claimed that young children should be introduced to the latest technology at school. _____ (8) Clearly, children can benefit from early exposure to technology. _____ (9) However, it is simply not true that the latest gadgets should be introduced in elementary schools. _SI_ (10) It is best to let children be children, and to introduce the world of technology when they are older.

---

2 Complete the sentences about distracted driving. Circle the words that correctly complete each sentence.

1. Distracted driving is a type of information overload. _____, trying to do two things at once overloads the brain.

   a. However   (b.) Clearly   c. It is not true that

2. _____ most drivers can safely talk on the phone or use a GPS while driving.

   (a.) It could be argued that   b. That may be so,   c. While it is true that

3. _____ that hands-free use of a cell phone is safer than hand-held use.

   a. Obviously,   b. However   c. It has been claimed

4. _____ using a hands-free device reduces one type of distraction, it does not eliminate the danger.

   a. While it is true that   b. Of course,   c. It might be claimed that

5. Some researchers have found that talking with a passenger in one's car is just as dangerous as talking on a phone, but _____ .

   a. other researchers disagree   b. it is not true that   c. it has been argued

6. _____ , a passenger can help the driver see danger, while a person at the other end of a phone call cannot.

   a. It could be claimed   b. It is not true that   c. Obviously

7. When it comes to texting and driving, _____ mostly young people are at fault, but research shows that people of all ages are using hand-held devices while driving.

   a. naturally   b. it could be claimed that   c. it is not true that

8. Many people think that they can do two things at once. _____ , that is probably not true.

   a. It is argued that   b. However   c. Some researchers disagree

3 Unscramble the sentences about information overload.

1. lead / important health information / individuals to ignore / information overload can / it is argued that

   It is argued that information overload can lead individuals to ignore
   important health information.

2. in an age with so many / clearly, / we are fortunate to live / sources of good health information

   _____

3. to an increase in good behaviors / can lead to an increase / naturally, / access to information / in awareness and therefore

   _____

4. lead to confusion / of information available online / can actually / however, / the huge volume

   _____

5. good health advice / when people are confused, / it has been argued that / they end up not benefiting from

   _____

6. it's hard to know / there are so many different recommendations about health that / which ones to follow / it has been claimed that

_____

7. one source making one claim / of course, information / and later research claiming the opposite / can be contradictory, with

_____

8. while it is true that / should be accessible to everyone / there is a link between education levels and beliefs about health, / good health information

_____

4 Think of what you have learned online about good health and staying well. On a separate piece of paper, write a short paragraph (four or five sentences) persuading people to practice a healthy habit or stop an unhealthy habit. Use common vocabulary that addresses opposing views.

Avoid Common Mistakes

1 Circle the mistakes.

1. You might be surprised **at the work** librarians **do today** (whether) you haven't visited a
   (a)   (b)   (c)
   library lately.

2. A librarian can help you **if** you are wondering **if or not** a source **has the information**
                          (a)   (b)   (c)
   you need.

3. Librarians respond **to all types of requests** for information, so they usually know
                      (a)
   weather or not a source is reliable.
    (b)   (c)

4. Librarians often **help visitors use the Internet whether** they are unfamiliar with
                    (a)   (b)   (c)
   searching for information online.

5. Librarians can help **you figure out** if or not a book or website has
                       (a)   (b)
   what you are looking for.
    (c)

6. Some people wonder wether or not librarians are still relevant **in today's world**.
                     (a)   (b)   (c)

7. In difficult times, local governments sometimes have **to decide** if or not libraries
                                                        (a)   (b)
   should be kept open.
    (c)   essential

8. Libraries are critical **whether** we **want modern information tools**
                         (a)   (b)
   to be accessible to everyone.
    (c)

2 Identify the common mistakes in the sentences. Label each sentence with the type of mistake from the box. If there is no mistake, write *d*. Then correct each mistake.

---

a. Remember to use *if*, and not *whether*, to express a condition.

b. Remember that *or not* can immediately follow *whether*, but it can only appear at the end of a sentence with *if*.

c. Remember to spell *whether* correctly.

d. There is no mistake.

_b_ How do you know ~~if~~ *whether* or not you are suffering from information overload? _c_ To
(1)   (2)

answer this question, it's a good idea to reflect on ~~weather~~ *whether* you frequently feel stressed,

or feel that you can't accomplish anything. _a_ You may be suffering from information
                                            (3)

overload ~~whether~~ *if* you frequently feel depressed or exhausted from staying in touch

electronically. E-mail can be a real source of anxiety. _d_ One agency calculated that
                                                        (4)

if it averaged all of its incoming e-mails for a single week, its employees received 250

e-mails per person every working day. _b_ For each message we receive, we have to
                                        (5)

decide ~~if~~ *whether* or not it needs an answer, can be deleted, or requires an action. _c_ Later, we
                                                                                          (6)

wonder ~~weather~~ *whether* we might have missed something important by acting so quickly. _d_
                                                                                             (7)

It's not known whether the constant flow of messages is harmful; some believe that it

makes us unable to focus on important tasks, and makes us less creative. _a_ ~~Whether~~ *if*
                                                                           (8)

this has happened to you, you might want to try some time management strategies.

_d_ Of course, you might ask yourself whether you would have preferred to live in
(9)

a time when people had too little information, instead of too much. Most likely, the

answer will be no!

Self-Assessment

Circle the word or phrase that correctly completes each sentence.

1. People need to think about _____ balance social networking websites and real-life situations in a healthy way.

   a. how they can   b. how can they   c. how can

2. _____ social networking websites are 100% safe. However, this is simply not true.

   a. It has been claimed that   b. While it is true that   c. Obviously

3. Corporations want to find out _____ social networking websites will help them attract more customers.

   a. if   b. while   c. can they

4. Some employers want to find out _____ reduce information overload in their employees.

   a. whether can   b. they if   c. how they can

5. Many companies wonder _____ benefit them.

   a. how can technology   b. technology can   c. how technology can

6. Shifts in technology happen quickly; it can be a challenge to know _____ .

   a. what the best choices are   b. what are the best choices   c. the best choices are

7. More research is needed on _____ best be used in the workplace and in education.

   a. how can technology   b. technology can   c. how technology can

8. Individuals need to decide _____ constantly accessible by phone, texts, and e-mail.

   a. what they want to be   b. they want to be   c. whether or not they want to be

9. From time to time, it's a good idea to ask yourself _____ too connected.

   a. if you are   b. whether or not you   c. are you

10. _____ by several researchers that Internet use, like TV watching, contributes to weight gain.

    a. It could be argued   b. It has been argued   c. It has argued

11. _____ we are lucky to live in the information age, it is still a good idea sometimes to just turn everything off and relax.

    a. However,   b. It is not true that   c. While it is true that

12. We depend on _____ and are fortunate to have access to so many sources.

    a. information of course   b. information, of course,   c. information of course,

13. _____ or not we handle information well is up to us.

    a. If   b. Whether   c. Weather

14. _____ you want to post your personal information on social networking websites is your decision, but check the sites' privacy policies before you do.

    a. Unless   b. If   c. Whether or not

15. According to the latest statistics, well over 800 million people in the world have a social networking account. _____ people have embraced this phenomenon.

    a. Possibly   b. Clearly,   c. However,

Persuasion 3
Social Networking

could, might, may – possibility
should, would – expectation

Expressing Future Actions

1 A Complete the sentences about social networking. Use the clues and modal verbs in parentheses. Sometimes more than one answer is possible.

1. Social networking sites *may/might/could lose* users if they continue current practices. (lose; possibility)

2. Advertisements on social networking sites *should* _____ a major issue soon, as users are becoming increasingly irritated by their presence. (become; expectation)

3. In fact, SNSs ___ *may / could* ___ unless there is less advertising. (disappear; possibility)

4. SNS users ___ *might* ___ viewing advertising messages in the future. (stop; possibility)

5. If social networking sites limit advertising messages, they ___ *would keep* ___ users. (keep; expectation based on condition)

6. In a recent study, many users reported that they *may/might/would* to pay to use SNSs if it would mean fewer ads. (be willing; expectation based on condition)

7. In the same study, a significant number of users said they *might / would* ___ SNSs if there is less advertising. (visit; possibility)

8. These survey results *should* _____ future advertising campaigns. (affect; expectation)

B Read the sentences in A again. Then answer the question.

Which sentences in A have more than one possible modal? _____ Write them next to the sentences.

2 Circle the words that best complete each sentence.

1. After months of research, we **are about** / **will** to unveil a new marketing plan.

2. We **intend to** / **are about** advertise on only one social networking site.

3. Therefore, we **are going to** / **anticipate** determine which site is the most popular with our potential customers.

4. Research indicates that one site **is going / is considering** to overtake all the other social networking sites in the near future.

5. We **will / anticipate** focusing on that site as opposed to any others.

6. We **will / seem likely** need a variety of ads on this one site.

7. For example, we **are going to / are considering** advertising in social networking games.

8. The reason is that the numbers of players of these online games **are likely / will** to increase dramatically in the near future.

3 Complete the paragraphs with the expressions in the box. Use each expression once. Change the form when necessary.

about	be likely to	due to	~~might be~~	seem likely
anticipate	consider	intend to	plan	

Some teachers think that it *might be* necessary to block students' access to social
(1)

networking sites in the future. However, we feel that teachers need to understand the

power of social networking as an educational tool. It _____ that social
(2)

networking is not going to disappear. In fact, it _____ grow in importance in
(3)

the near future. Therefore, schools should _____ exploiting social networking
(4)

instead of banning it.

We are _____ to unveil several new programs at our school that use
(5)

social networking. We will employ social networking tools in several different ways. For

example, the English department _____ maximize the beneficial aspects of
(6)

social networking for communicating with others. Starting next semester, the instructors

_____ to use blogs for writing assignments. This will motivate students by
(7)

giving them the opportunity to have a range of people view and respond to their work.

Our colleagues are likely to find other ways to use social networking as an educational

tool. In fact, the math department is _____ announce a social networking
(8)

program in a few days. We look forward to these changes and _____ having
(9)

great success with these new programs.

4 Answer the questions. Write sentences that are true for you. Use the expression in bold in your answers.

1. What do you **plan to** study in school?

   I plan to study architecture.

2. What do you **hope to** do after you graduate?

   _____

3. What changes, if any, do you **intend to** make in the near future?

   _____

4. What job would you **consider** doing in the future?

   _____

5. What **are** you **likely to** do when you finish school?

   _____

Common Words and Phrases in Persuasive Writing

1 Complete the sentences about social networking sites and communication. Circle the word that correctly completes each sentence.

1. (**Proponents**)/ **Opponents** of social networking sites argue that these communities strengthen relationships.

2. **Opponents / Advocates** of blogging make the claim that it promotes free speech.

3. It is **true / incomplete** that social networking is a useful tool for communication.

4. The main **argument / problem** used by supporters of social networking is that these communities bring like-minded people together.

5. **Supporters / Opponents** of social media claim that these sites are not good for relationships because they reduce the amount of face-to-face communication that people have.

6. Opponents of social media make the **claim / evidence** that these sites are bad for business because many employees access the sites at work.

7. **Proponents / Opponents** of social networking believe that it is a tool for positive social change.

8. Most parents **estimate / support** increased privacy controls on social media sites.

9. Some experts **advocate / believe** monitoring children's use of social networking.

10. However, others **oppose / argue** supervising their online behavior.

11. Opponents of monitoring **argue / refute** that children have the right to privacy.

12. Ruiz **claims / refutes** the notion that children have the right to privacy.

13. Smith's argument about teenagers and the concept of privacy is **valid / incomplete**. She fails to refer to recent literature on adolescent psychology.

14. Green's argument is unproven because there is **little / true** evidence for his claim.

15. Yee's conclusion is **illogical / better** because it is based on ideas that are not true.

2 Unscramble the words to complete the sentences about students' use of laptops. Then check (✓) the statements that are in favor of students using laptops in the classroom.

<u>✓</u> 1. to / order / take / in / notes

Proponents of the idea claim that some students

need laptops in class *in order to take notes* .

_____ 2. idea / opponents / to / the / of / according

_____ , laptops
encourage cheating because students
can look up answers.

_____ 3. the / argument / used / that / by / main / proponents / of / idea / the / is

_____ laptops help students with poor organizational skills.

_____ 4. students / laptops / distract / claim / can / the / that

_____ is a common argument used by opponents.

_____ 5. of / the / idea / arguments / of / one / against / main / the

_____ using laptops in class is that students are not paying full attention.

_____ 6. claim / favor / that / idea / people / are / the / in / who / of

_____ laptops help students organize important information.

_____ 7. students / that / the / fact / to / due

Advocates of using laptops in the classroom argue that class time is used more efficiently

_____ can look things up instead of interrupting the teacher.

_____ 8. believe / opponents / that / the / of / idea

_____ students can be distracted by the noise of typing or the light on the screens.

Avoid Common Mistakes

1 Circle the mistakes.

1. The (**claiming**) that social networking sites **could** disappear within the next five years
   (a)   (b)
   is **illogical**.
      (c)

2. The administration **will consider** the **arguing** that social networking **is affecting**
                      (a)   (b)   (c)
   students' grades.

3. **Proponents** of the **claiming** that laptops in the classroom are a disturbance **might**
   (a)   (b)   (c)
   have a good point.

4. **According for** a recent report, a large university **is about to** **require** laptops for all
   (a)   (b)   (c)
   entering students.

5. **It seems likely** that a certain number of students **might not agree** with the **claiming**
   (a)   (b)   (c)
   that using social networking sites leads to lower grades.

6. Students **anticipate** **spending** less time online next semester, **according with** a
              (a)   (b)   (c)
   campus survey.

7. **Proponents** of laptops in the classroom **use** the **arguing** that laptops help students
   (a)   (b)   (c)
   take notes.

8. The **arguing** that parents **can** completely control their children's online access
       (c)   (b)
   is **invalid**.
      (c)

2 Identify the common mistakes in the sentences. Label each sentence with the type of mistake from the box. If there is no mistake, write *d*. Then correct each sentence.

> a. Do not confuse the noun and verb form of *claim*.
> b. Do not confuse the noun and verb form of *argue*.
> c. Remember to use *according to*, and not *according for* or *according with*.
> d. There is no mistake.

SNSs and College

≪ previous | index | next ≫

arguments

b One of the main ~~arguing~~ in favor of social networking sites is that they provide an
(1)

easy way for organizations to communicate with individuals. ____ In fact, according with
(2)

a recent report, over 80 percent of colleges and universities in the United States are using

social networking sites to recruit new students and to keep in touch with former students.

____ In addition, according to the same study, colleges are now using SNSs as part of
(3)

the admission process. ____ Proponents of using social networking sites for college
(4)

admissions argue that it helps them make decisions when there are many equally qualified

candidates. ____ However, their claiming that this is a useful source of information on
(5)

prospective students is invalid. ____ This is because SNSs often contain false information.
(6)

____ For example, according for a recent study, people are much more likely to lie online
(7)

than they are in face-to-face contact. ____ According for the study, people feel that they
(8)

can get away with lying online because there is no immediate reaction to the lie, as there

would be in face-to-face communication. ____ Another arguing against the use of SNSs in
(9)

college admissions is that it is impossible to know who the actual author of a site is. ____
(10)

False social networking pages can be created to make false claims and spread incorrect

information about an individual. ____ In fact, according with a survey of admissions
(11)

officers, colleges often receive anonymous links to sites with negative information on other

applicants. ____ Whether these sites are genuine or not, this supports the argument that
(12)

they should not be used in the college admissions process.

Self-Assessment

Circle the word or phrase that correctly completes each sentence.

1. We predict that students' grades _____ once we ban access to SNSs.

   a. consider improving   b. improve   c. will improve

2. Experts predict that the popularity of SNSs _____ grow in the future.

   a. likely   b. will   c. anticipate

3. Students are _____ class time checking SNS updates if we do not block access on campus.

   a. going to spend   b. will spend   c. due to spend

4. Without the ban, teachers _____ have to ban laptops in the classroom if they want students to pay attention.

   a. are likely   b. should   c. would

5. We are confident that the proposed rule _____ discourage students from bringing their laptops to class.

   a. would   b. might   c. seems likely

6. We are sure that spending less time on SNSs _____ improve students' grades.

   a. could   b. might   c. should

7. The college _____ unveil a new policy regarding laptops.

   a. is about to   b. intends   c. anticipates

8. The social networking site _____ creating a new privacy policy in the next few months.

   a. is due to   b. is about to   c. anticipates

9. It _____ that more schools will use social networking for educational purposes.

   a. is like   b. seems likely   c. is likely to

10. The company is _____ monitoring employees' Internet use.

    a. considering   b. anticipates   c. is about to

11. Some parents _____ that children should be supervised while they are online.

    a. intend to   b. believe   c. are in favor of

12. Some parents _____ blocking inappropriate websites.

    a. are in favor of   b. argue   c. claim

13. The _____ that colleges need to use social networking sites to evaluate students is illogical.

    a. claimed   b. claim   c. claiming

14. According _____ a recent report, many colleges are using social networking sites to find new students.

   a. to   b. with   c. for

15. Some educators argue that social networking use is distracting for students, but we disagree with this _____ .

   a. claiming   b. claims   c. claim